Rama Chandra Ghosha

The Indo Aryans

Their History, Creed and Practice

Rama Chandra Ghosha

The Indo Aryans
Their History, Creed and Practice

ISBN/EAN: 9783742837462

Manufactured in Europe, USA, Canada, Australia, Japa

Cover: Foto ©Thomas Meinert / pixelio.de

Manufactured and distributed by brebook publishing software
(www.brebook.com)

Rama Chandra Ghosha

The Indo Aryans

THE INDO-ARYANS,

THEIR HISTORY, CREED AND PRACTICE.

BY

RAMACHANDRA GHOSHA. F.R.S.L.

MEMBER OF THE ROYAL ASIATIC SOCIETY, LONDON.

———

CALCUTTA :

B. BANERJEE & CO., 25-27, CORNWALLIS STREET.

———

1881.

TO

THE REV. K. M. BANERJEA, LL. D.,

HON. M. R. A. S., F. R. C.,

HONORARY CHAPLAIN TO THE BISHOP OF CALCUTTA,

WHO OCCUPIES A CONSPICUOUS POSITION AMONG THE EMINENT
SCHOLARS OF THE DAY, AND WHO HAS PLACED THE
STUDENT OF VAIDIK LITERATURE UNDER DEEP AND LASTING
OBLIGATION BY HIS RECENT SUCCESSFUL ATTEMPT TO
ESTABLISH THE RELATION BETWEEN THE RIG-VEDA
AND THE ASSYRIAN INSCRIPTIONS,

THIS VOLUME

IS DEDICATED AS A SINCERE MARK OF PROFOUND REGARD
AND DEEP GRATITUDE,

BY HIS AFFECTIONATE FRIEND,

THE AUTHOR.

PREFACE

The precise object of the following pages is to present to the reader certain facts regarding the history, creed and practice of the Indo-Aryans, as far as these can be obtained from a study of ancient Sanskrit Literature. In taking up such extensive and complicated subjects I had to work up the materials which I had collected for many years; and these materials often so much embarrassed me by their copiousness and diversity that I had little hope of benefiting from them. There is, indeed, a dense mist of prejudice and preconceived opinions which always impede such investigations. But it should be frankly stated that great advances have since been made in the field of Sanskrit research, though much remains to ascertain and unsettled as before. The laborers in the field have now greatly increased; and their researches reflect lasting honor upon them. I need not give their names here when I have referred to them so frequently in the text and in the foot-notes; but I should only acknowledge with deep gratitude that I have greatly availed myself of their writings.

The Vedas are the gigantic labors of the Hindu mind. They have already attracted the attention of some of the best scholars of Europe and America. They are guidebooks in all researches into the civilization of the ancient Hindus, on which history cannot throw the least light; though it must be admitted that the information to be gleaned from them is very scanty. Indeed, India never produced a Xenophon or a Thucydides;

but nevertheless history can be built up from the materials which lie buried in these ancient documents, by simply distinguishing facts from the shoals of mystical legends and mythological drapery which are found to envelop them. The age in which the Vedas and their appendages were composed, has exercised the blandest influence upon all succeeding periods of Indian history ; every later branch of literature is closely connected with the Vaidik traditions ; the religious and moral ideas have been derived from them ; the later mythology has also developed out of them ; and the Hindu life, in all its aspects, has been moulded by old traditionary precepts.

Though the researches of occidental savans into the Vedas are alike profound and accurate, they carry us into a labyrinth of heterogeneous materials, which to digest and at last to present in a readable shape is indeed a hard task. The general deductions and opinions of one Sanskritist in the West are in some cases not found to tally with those of his brother Sanskritist. Thus in many cases they, far from helping us to attain the truth, often throw great doubts and confusion on many an important and salient point. I have, therefore, generally avoided mixing issues with them whenever I happened to find myself to differ widely from any one of them on such controverted points, and have only tried to arrive at a definite conclusion whenever that was possible. To claim to have certainly arrived at a literary truth is highly presumptuous in a country such as we live in, where the spirit of Niebuhr has not as yet been attained.

At all events their contributions towards ancient Sanskrit Literature have elucidated many knotty problems ; which could never have been solved by the Indian Pandits, who hardly possess a scientific turn of mind ; and have at last brought to our knowledge an immense store of information of vital importance which had been so long hid from us by the dishonorable attempts of the Brahmans, who debarred all but themselves from reading the Vedas. It is, however, a curious commentary on the vicissitudes of human affairs that the proud descendants of the holy Rishis should consume their midnight oil on the banks of the Ganges, over their sacred books, published for the first time on the banks of the Neckar and the Thames, by those, whom they look upon as Mlechhas.

My warmest thanks are due to my esteemed friend the Hon'ble Pyārimohana Mukhopādhyāya, of Uttarapara, for kindly placing at my disposal various books and manuscripts a reference to which was necessary in preparing these pages for publication.

R. G.

CALCUTTA, May, 1881.

CONTENTS.

THE INDO-ARYANS.

CHAPTER I.

The Earliest History of the Indo-Aryan Family.

CENTRAL ASIA was probably the earliest point of ethnic movement, the homestead of the human family, the common abode of those races which have hitherto guided the van of civilization. The languages and mythologies of almost all the great historic races, however now widely separated, beckon to that country as their common dwelling place. Amidst the recesses of that focus of radiation and cradle of historic races, lie the materials of forty centuries of human history. When such dubious half-blind guides as mythology and tradition fail to penetrate into what lie in the pre-historic deeps, the languages can only with scientific certainty point out the way. So comparative Philology has been very appropriately called linguistic Palæontology. A study of the morphology and grammar of the Sanskrit in its oldest form, and of the Celtic, Greek, Latin, Lettish, Slavonic and Persian, shows us that all these languages sprung out of the same parent tongue, now extinct. It follows, therefore, as a necessary corollary that the nations, which spoke these languages,

were also descended from one and the same stock ; and they
once constituted one united people.* Affinity in language
certainly affords some presumption of affinity in race ; but
it is not in languages alone that an affinity exists between
the Indians, the Iranians, the Greeks, and the Romans ;
their mythologies also imply a community of origin, and
no doubt they yield some data for ethnic deductions. At
any rate, the cradle of the Indo-Aryans is to be sought
for in some country external to India ; and the facts
which have been brought to light enable us to determine
the region in which the whole Aryan family must have
lived together.

The Aryans, in the childhood of their history, were
savages ; and lived upon the flesh of wild animals which
they hunted. They had not even huts to live in ; but generally
formed a small gang either for protecting themselves from
dangers to which they were naturally exposed ; or for hunt-
ing wild beasts for the purpose of food. They gradually
passed to pastoral life ; pastures now formed their territory
and cattle their wealth. They soon acquired quiet and
harmless habits, and became sober and diligent. They
also became encircled by large families. In this manner,
a number of clans were formed ; and the gotra system is
founded on a division into such clans. The shepherd easily
became the leader of his clan ; while the hunter, as a more
adventurer, could not take the lead, because his influence
over his gang was by no means permanent. They now
carried on agriculture and developed it ; and also ap-
propriated permanent property in the land. They con-

* Weber a Indische Skizzen. p 7

structed permanent habitations; and their diet was much
improved. Chivalry is, in fact, the outgrowth of a
desire of luxury; and the necessity of self-defence pro-
motes the growth of feudalism. After thus passing
through many vicissitudes of fortune they gradually formed
themselves into a feudal community governed by the
same religious and social institutions, and the same political organization. Small states were thus formed; and
there is no doubt that the Indo-Aryans reached this stage
of civilization before they immigrated into India. But
when they advanced from one stage of civilization to another
they did by no means give up all their former institutions
and customs; nor did they discard the religious and social
polity, to which they had once become attached.

The pre-emigration events as recorded in the *Rig-
veda*, which again are confirmed by the Zend-Avesta and
the Assyrian Inscriptions, and by a legend in the Satapatha-Brāhmaṇa (i. 2, 5, § 6), naturally point to the west
of Asia for the primitive home of the Aryans; and also
to the migratory route of the Indo-Aryans and the
Perso-Aryans from " the West to the East." Our ancestors as well speak of their "old home," the *pratna okas*;"
but cannot give its geography. In the *Rig-veda* an expression also occurs which might lead us to suppose that the
Indo-Aryans still retained some reminiscences of their having at one time occupied a colder country.† And in the
allusions made to the northerly region of the Uttarakurus
there may be some recollections of their early connexion

* Rig-veda, i. 30, 9.
† Rig-veda, i. 64, 14; v. 54, 15; vi. 10, 7; vi. 12, 6; vi. 13, 6; vi. 17, 15.

with the countries to the north of the Himálayas.[*] Ptolemy (Geogr. vi. 16) was also acquainted with the Uttarakuru. According to Lassen the Ottorokora (οττοροκόρα) of Ptolemy must be sought for to the east of Kashghar. There is again a tradition in the First Fargard of the Vendidád regarding the earliest abodes of the Aryan race. The description contained in it is simply of the gradual diffusion or rather of the first sixteen settlements of the Aryan race. The Airyana-vaêjô is first spoken of in it; but its locality is not mentioned, nor is its geography given. It means the Aryan residence; and by it we are to understand the original country of the Aryans. We have here undoubtedly geographical descriptions of some real countries. Of the sixteen lands alluded to nine did certainly exist; and we know their geographical positions. The Airyana-vaêjô could be localised in the basin of the Araxes which was identified with the Oxus in the time of Herodotus. However, the admission of the praise also on the part of our ancestors shows clearly that they came to India from beyond the Indus; and moreover the testimonies which have been brought to light point to Media as that home, the officina gentium whence issued swarms of men whose descendants now constitute the most civilised nations of the earth; and the migration of those men apparently belongs to a period far beyond the reach of documentary history. Afterwards a Turanian invasion of Media was probably the cause of the gradual dispersion of the whole family on all sides. They must have travelled away from their primeval abodes, at different times, and in different direc-

[*] Aitareya-Bráhmana, vol. 14. Weber's Indische Studien, i. p. 218.

tions. It is not, however, easy to define their routes; some of
course went westward, others eastward.* Those that went
westward were the first to break off from their pristine home;
and those that came eastward were the last of the emigrants.
Probably after many defections in the course of their
migration some of them may have remained behind, and
established themselves in different countries. But those
that came eastward had to encounter on their way the con-
flicts which are recorded in the Veda and the Zand-Avesta;
and this also receives confirmation from the temporary disap-
pearance of Vishnu from them in their marches. Their
marches were, no doubt, something like religious processions
regularly worshipping and performing their ceremonial
acts, the rear and flank guards repeating hymns in the
Vaidik seven metres,† and the vanguard bearing the holy
fire in the front.‡

After crossing the narrow passes of the Hindukush, the
eastern branch first settled on the north-western frontiers
of India, in the Panjáb, and even beyond the Panjáb on the
Kubhá.§ In the Panjáb they continued to form one community for a considerable time ‖ and they lived on equal
terms so far as the worship of the Sun and Fire and
the elements of Nature was concerned. They had also
the primitive institution of sacrifices; though they differed among themselves as to their scope and the mode

* Banerjea's Arian Witness, p. 111.
† Rig-veda, I. 22, 16.
‡ Muir's Sanskrit Texts, iv. 122.
§ Weber's Indische Studien, iv. p. 379, n.
‖ Müller's Last Results of the Persian Researches, p. 113, and his Lec-
tures on the Science of Language, i. p. 226.

of conducting them. But one party insisted on the actual completion of the sacrifice as the *Vashat* ; while the other would not allow it. Nor would the latter sanction even the use of the Soma drink by which the former set store.[*] There were also some principal doctrinal differences between both the parties ; and such religious differences only separated the one from the other.[†] There are certainly historical allusions to the schism both in the Veda and in the Avesta. But according to Haug the causes of the schism were not only of a religious but also of a social and political nature.[‡] And both the parties latterly formed again two other branches, the Indo-Aryans and the Persu-Aryans. Now each branch bore feelings of bitterness against the other ; and many were the sanguinary conflicts which took place between them. It also appears from the Rig-veda that Ishtava or the Sanskrit transliteration of Vishtaspa of the Zend-Avesta, who was the patron of Zoroaster[§] and the promoter of his doctrines, had contemplated the forcible imposition of his prophet's teaching on all around him by fire and sword.[|] But the ancestors of the Indo-Aryans refused manfully to submit to such religious intolerance ; and they strenuously defended their own religion. "What can Ishtava," said they, "what can Ishtarasmi, rulers of the world as they are, do against our

[*] Yasna, xxxii 3 ; xlviii 10 ; see also Haug's Essays, p. 291.

[†] Bleeck, Introduction to the Avesta, p. x ; Weller's Last Results of the Persian Researches, p. 113 ; and his Chips from a German Workshop, i. p. 83

[‡] Haug's Essays, p. 292

[§] In the Rig-veda (viii. 87, 7) this name appears in the corrupt form of Jamdashti.

[|] Farvardin-yast, xiii. 90.

protecting men !"* As to who this Vishtáspa was we are
still in the dark, but he must have been different from the
father of Darius, as he was a more ancient character.

Bhrigu originated pyro-cultus (*Rig-veda,* i. 58, 6 ; i.
60, 1 ; x. 122, 5), and promoted the celebration of sacrificial ceremonies in the world at large ; and there can be
no doubt that our ancestors, who composed the eastern
branch of the Aryan race, were originally Fire-worshippers
(i. 1, 2). They also no doubt recognised two principles, one
the supreme principle of Good and the other the principle
of Evil. In the Zand-Avesta the supreme principle of
Good is called Ahura Mazda, which means the *all-knowing
or wise Lord.* This name precisely corresponds with Asura-
prachetá (iv. 55, 1) in the *Rig-veda.* And Angró-mainyush,
the spirit of Evil or Sin in the Zand-Avesta, is also identical
with Nirriti (i. 24, 9) of the Veda. But here it should
be candidly stated that, according to the Zand-Avesta,
Ahura Mazda and Angró-mainyush are independent creators of good and evil respectively ; while, according to
the Veda, Nirriti is not "an uncreate eternal substance."†
In the Assyrian empire Asur was an appellative for God ;
and the eastern branch may have accepted the term from
the Assyrians. In the older portions of the *Rig-veda* the
appellative is used in as good a sense as in the Zand-Avesta ;
and so we find the Maruts (i. 64, 2), Indra (i. 54, 3),
Varuna. (ii. 27, 10), Tvashtri (i. 110, 3), Agni (v. 12–1),
Váyu (v. 42, 1), Púshan (v. 51, 11), Savitri (v. 49, 2),
Parjanya (v. 63. 3, 7), and other gods termed or accosted

* *Rig-veda,* i. 122, 13.
† Banerjea's Essays, p. 52.

as Asuras. But in these portions again the epithet is used, though only twice, in a bad sense (ii. 32, 4 ; vii. 99, 5) i. e. evil spirits or obstructors of religious rites and ceremonies. The term Asura was also applicable both to the Assyrian nation and to the follower of Ahura Mazda. Again, the Indo-Aryans were called Daêvas in the Zend-Avesta, and the Zoroastrians were in like manner called Asuras in the Veda. The term Asura, in its bad sense, was either intended for the Assyrians as a nation or for the intolerant Zoroastrians. And thus the contradictory senses of the name can only be accounted for by the fact that either because there arose the odium theologicum between the Indo-Aryans and the Pers-Aryans, or because the Indo-Aryans had national antipathy for they had the bitter recollections of the barbarous atrocities which the Assyrian kings boastingly practised against them when they once lived under the yoke of Assyria (Asur).

They must have penetrated into India not all at once, but in successive waves of immigration. The Indo-Aryans, after the Pers-Aryans had separated from them, and migrated westward to Arachosia and Persia, (in this period the Aryan mind blended with the Semitic, and no doubt it was the most momentous period in their history which surely opened another stage of religious thought) gradually spread towards the east, beyond the Sarasvatî, and over Hindustan as far as the Ganges ;* and afterwards diffused themselves to the south of the peninsula. Many centuries were of course required to subjugate the wild and vigorous aborigines, to break down their residences, and to

* Weber's Indische Studien, II p. 32.

bring them over to Brahmanism. The Indo-Aryans
so isolated themselves from their primitive settlement as
to have lost in a very short time all sympathy for their
cousins. And after they had got a home in India, they
began to ignore all trans-Indus events, and to declare
themselves as the autochthones of Indian soil.[*] In India
they must have established themselves by household
groups, each occupying a specifically assigned area within
the boundaries of which the intruders were only allowed
to settle upon terms of subjection. Though bound together by the feelings of a common descent, language and
religion, and by their joint hostility to the aborigines,
they were divided into clans quite separate from one another. They were now communities of free men. In such
a state the position of an individual member was as the head
of a family and the master of wealth.[†] Now they stood
in constant alarm of the aborigines ; and they were often
engaged in hostilities with them, and even with the members of their own community, simply with a view to be
enriched with the booty.[‡] The country they now occupied
was partly cultivated, and partly covered by forests. And
it was no doubt peopled by various tribes,[§] and divided
into numerous principalities.[‖]

At such primitive times when they were all a pastoral
and agricultural people, there could exist no distinct caste

[*] Banerjea's Arian Witness, pp. 39, 41.
[†] Whitney's Oriental and Linguistic Studies, p. 23.
[‡] Rig-veda, I. 73, 5.
[§] Roth's Literature and History of the Veda, pp. 131, ff.
[‖] Wilson's Rig-veda, I. p. xlii.

of cultivators of the earth ; when they were all warriors there could be no military caste ; and when each member of the community had the privilege to approach the gods with his own prayers and offerings there could be no sacerdotal order. Then the castes had no existence. At the time when the Indo-Aryans left their original home, and set foot on Indian soil, they naturally came into contact with the Dasyus or the aborigines of India. These people, forming the Turanian branch of the human family, differed widely from the Indo-Aryans, in their physical appearance and color, language and manners. Under such divergence, there was no ground for the establishment or conservation of feelings of amity and unity between the classes. Consequently, the Indo-Aryans and the Dasyus frequently found themselves in the bitterest conflict. The Indo-Aryans, as they were naturally of fair complexion, of majestic appearance, civilised and much more advanced in thought, looked down upon the aborigines who were of beastly appearance. In the Veda, the aborigines are frequently called Dasyus or Dāsas ;[*] and the Indo-Aryans, with a certain degree of hatred, called them *tuacham krish-ntm*[†] or the "blackskin." From the Veda, we obtain sufficient evidence of there having been a wide difference and natural enmity between them ; and the Indo-Aryans are found scornfully to apply to the Dasyus the terms of *anrata* (vi. 14, 3.), *apavrata* (v. 42, 9.), *ayajyu* (i. 131, 4.) *abrahma* (iv. 16, 9.), *anindra* (i. 133, 1.), etc. The

* Ṛig-veda, i. 102, 3 ; i. 117, 21 ; vi. 25, 2, 3 ; vi. 60, 6 ; vii. 63, 1 ; x. 36, 3 ; x. 96, 19 ; x. 102, 3 ; x. 63, 1.

† Ṛig-veda, i. 130, 8 ; ix. 41, 1.

main difference consisted in color and feature ; and hence varna gradually came to imply caste. Caste then was purely an ethnological institution. In the Veda varna appears in the sense of color (i. 73, 7 ; i. 113, 3), of bright color or light (iii. 34, 5), and of race, the white and the dark (ii. 12, 4 ; iii. 34, 8, 9).

In several places of the Rig-veda, five classes are generally spoken of such as pancha-krishtayah, pancha-kshitayah, pancha-charshanayah, pancha-janah, pancha-bhúma, and pancha-játa. There is no clue to be found for the better understanding of what tribal divisions or social classifications these classes implied. Mankind, in a collective sense, are said to be distinguished into five classes. Sáyana, following the received tradition of his own time, explains these terms as denoting the four castes with the Nishádas or the aborigines for a fifth. Yáska, in Nirukta (iii. 8), referring to the opinions of older schools, says that these five classes of beings are the Gandharvas, Pitris, Devas, Asuras, and Rakshasas, and according to some the four castes, and the aborigines or Nishádas. But these meanings seem quite immaterial, and are merely imaginary. When the five classes are designated by so many distinct appellatives, and especially by such a one as pancha-bhúma, it appears that these classifications arose possibly from the different localities the Indo-Aryans first occupied after their advent to India. The authors of the hymns of the Rig-veda regarded Manu as the common progenitor of the whole of the Aryan people, either the priests or the chiefs, or those that formed the mass of the population.[*] This

* Rig-veda, i. 80, 16 ; i. 114, 3 ; ii. 33, 13 ; iii. 3.2, 1 ; viii. 30 3

notion of descent from one common father overthrows
altogether the supposition that the Aryan nation originally
consisted of four different castes.

From the mass of the population were formed in course of
time two privileged classes, a priesthood and an aristocracy.
But after the population had greatly increased a division
of labor soon became a necessity. The more contemplative among them betook themselves to the worship of
the gods, and to the performance of rites and ceremonies
at the holy altars; the more powerful class held rule over
the rest; and the majority of the population followed various occupations; while the aborigines incorporated themselves in the Indo-Aryan community either as slaves[*] or
as handicraftsmen. The priesthood was formed only from
the employment by the chiefs of individuals known for
their rhythmical faculty, knowledge of sacred things, and
sanctity, to officiate at the worship of the gods; and the
aristocracy was formed properly from the class of petty
kings. The families of these kings who held sway over
single tribes came gradually to occupy a more and more
prominent position in the larger kingdoms which were of
necessity founded; and thus the military caste was formed.
And the people proper, the vicas, formed a third caste.
The term Vaisya does not occur in any other hymns of the
Rig-veda, but in the Purusha-sûkta; and only once in the
Atharvan (v. 17, 9). The Vaisya formed the mass of the
people; the word being derived from vis which means
the general community. But the Sûdras were a mixed
body, partly composed of the aborigines themselves, partly

* Rig-veda, vii. 44, 22; Vâlakhilya 4, 2.

of those Aryans who had settled earlier in India, and partly
of those recruits from the later Aryan emigrants who threw
off the Brahmanical yoke.[*] But the condition of the Śûdras
was not so wretched then as it was afterwards. They were
allowed to attend the ceremonies; and they even took an
active part on such occasions. The Rig and the Atharva
vedas throw an immense blaze of light on the relations of
the different classes of Indian society to one another at the
time when they were formed. From the later hymns of
the Rig-veda we learn that the priesthood had already become a profession; but there are other indications also
which justify the conclusion that there was no discrimination
of profession; and even there are numerous references to be
found in all parts of the hymn-collection to a variety of
ranks, classes and professions however without any rigid
prescriptions about them. The three highest castes stood
in a more intimate relation with one another either in point
of descent or culture, than any of them did to the fourth.

We have, however, no knowledge of the political condition of the Indo-Aryans, beyond the specification of
the names of some princes. These names are peculiar to
the Veda. We have particular mention, not only of
kings, but of envoys (I. 127, 9) and heralds (ii. 127, 10).
The kings sent ambassadors to one another (I. 71, 4);
and also employed spies. The political institutions of
those days very closely resembled those of the Homeric
Greeks. The names for king meant father of the house,
and headman of the tribe. Each state was governed by

* Both's Literature and History of the Veda, p. 117; Weber's History
of Indian Literature, p. 18.

a king, whose office was often hereditary ; but also sometimes elective. Kings are mentioned in the hymns ;[*] and
rulers or governors under the titles of pârapatî[†] and grâ-
maṇî[‡] are also alluded to. These rulers held powers subject to certain obligations towards a king. The existence
of the office of kings, and the imposition of taxes (i.
70, 5), or contributions from the people for the mainten-
ance of kingdoms certainly imply a settled state of government. The government was good;[§] and even the village
system existed during that period. Meetings of princes
are alluded to (x. 97, 6). The princes were always surrounded by faithful friends (i. 73, 3); and they always took
delight in listening to the bards (i. 37, 18). There were
also halls of justice (ii. 134, 7) ; and the complicated law
of inheritance (iii. 31, 1-2) was to a certain extent in
force ; and our ancestors had conceptions of the rights
of property and definite guarantees for their preservation,
had formalities for transactions of exchange and sale (iii.
24, 9), for payment of wages, and for the administra-
tion of oath. (A. V. iv. 16). The laws of contract were
developed. Debts and debtors are even adverted to (ii. 24,
13 ; ii. 28, 9) ; and sometimes exorbitant interest was
charged (iii. 53, 14). The tricks of trade were also known
in those days.

Their chief possessions were the flocks and herds ; but
they by no means neglected the cultivation of the earth.

* Rig-veda. i. 40, 8 : i. 126, 1 ; iii. 43, 5 ; v. 27, 4 ; x. 33, 6.
† Ibid, i. 173, 10.
‡ Ibid, x. 62, 11.
§ Ibid, i. 173.

Cultivated and fertile lands (iii. 41, 6 ; iv. 20, 1) and water-courses are alluded to ;* and the irrigation of lands under cultivation is also recommended (ii. 122, 6). They sunk wells (i. 30, 1), and dug channels (ii. 28, 5). They measured their fields with rods (i. 110, 5). Oxen ploughed their fields (vi. 20, 19); and the articles of food were brought home in waggons and carts. We read of a husbandman repeatedly ploughing the earth for barley (i. 23, 15). They had also granaries (ii. 14, 11).

They had pasturage (i. 67, 3); and domesticated the cow, the sheep, the goat, the horse, and the dog. And the zoology of the Rig-veda comprises a great many other animals, such as lions, tigers, bears, wolves, elephants, oxen, camels, deers, antelopes, hogs, asses, rams, bulls, serpents, mosquitoes, bees, mares, scorpions, worms, snakes, flukes, crocodiles, porpoises, apes, owls, boars, buffaloes, jackals, mice, foxes, frogs, rats, and different kinds of birds, i. e. peacocks, eagles, pigeons, vultures, ducks, swans, kites, crows, quails, falcons, etc.

The community consisted of the rich and the poor.† The rich were no doubt over-bearing (i. 143, 2) ; and the middle classes pursued their trades and lived in comfort. But the lower classes lived from hand to mouth (iv. 25, 6). Labor was valued (i. 79, 1) ; and the spirit of adventure and enterprise was also appreciated (i. 17, 31). The different occupations pursued were those of priests, poets, physicians, barbers, wood-cutters, carpenters, black-smiths, female grinders of corn, carriage builders, workers in wood and metal, manufacturers of weapons of war and other sharp-

* Rig-veda, III. 43, 3 ; x. 43, 7.
† Ibid. x. 117.

edged implements, boat and ship builders, rope makers, and butchers. The bhisty with his skin brought them water; and the groom rubbed down their horses (ii. 135, 5).

They thought of the means of transit from the earliest times. They had good and great roads (i. 116, 20), suitable and little paths (i. 58, 1; iv. 16, 3) easy to be traversed in mountainous regions and inaccessible places. At the resting-places on the road refreshments were always kept ready (B. 166, 9). They navigated in oared boats (ii. 131, 2) and ferries.* They were a maritime and mercantile nation; sea-going ships and navigation in the open sea were familiar to them. They were not content with internal trade; they also undertook sea-voyages as we read of merchants sailing for gain.† Metal money had been in use; nishkas of gold being mentioned.‡ The use of money in trade may not have been unknown, for "merchants desirous of gain" are cited in the Rik, as sending their ships to the sea.§ We also read of swarnas; and a swarna, according to Colebrooke, was equal to sixteen nishkas. They were not only familiar with the oceans; but sometimes must have engaged in naval expeditions.‖ And there is mention made of a naval expedition under Bhujyu, the son of Tugra, against a foreign island, which was frustrated only by shipwreck. (i. 116, 3—5).

---

* Ṛig-veda, ii. 37.
† Ibid, i. 267.
‡ Ibid, i. 126. According to Manu (vii. 134) a nishka was a weight of gold equal to four swarnas. Yaska, in his Nirukta, p. 13, quotes from the Veda, eighteen different words, which convey the abstract idea of wealth, without having any reference to grain, or cattle, or any other object.
§ Ṛig-veda, i. 48, 3; i. 56, 2.
‖ Ibid, i. 116, 3.

There were cities (pur) as distinct from villages (grâ-ma).[*] We read of "cities of stone," of "cities made of iron,"[†] and of cities with a hundred surrounding walls,[‡] which convey the idea of forts consisting of a series of concentric walls. When we read of iron cities we should take them as more substantial than wattle and mud.

They lived in permanent habitations ; and their houses were roofed, and had windows and doors (i.113,4). Generally their houses were guarded by dogs. Bricks (ishtakâ) were made and known ; and lime, mortar, and stucco were used for the purpose of plastering them (iv. 47, 3). The words which occur in the Veda signifying a house attest to the existence of brick and stone buildings. We read of a "house having a thousand doors,"[§] of "a palace sup-ported by a thousand columns,"[‖] of "stately mansion" (i. 101, 8), of "lowly dwelling" (i. 101, 8), of a "destitute dwelling" (i. 104, 7), of the "spacious dwelling-place" (i. 84, 8), of "stone houses," of "carved stones," and of "brick edifices." There were also halls "vast, comprehensive and thousand-doored." Vasishtha longs for a "three storied dwelling" (v. 101, 8) ; and Atri is said to have been "thrown into a machine room with a hundred doors where he was roasted" (i. 51, 3).

They lived together with their sons and grandsons ; and their domestic economy was founded upon the principles

* Rig-veda, i. 114. 1 ; i. 44, 10 ; i. 49, 6 ; x. 104, 1.

† Ibid, i. 58, 8; ii. 85, 8 ; iv. 27, 1 ; vi. 3, 7 ; vii. 15, 14 ; vii. 95, 1 ; vii. 99, 8 ; x. 101, 8.

‡ Ibid, i. 166, 8 ; vii. 15, 14.

§ Ibid, vii. 88, 5.

‖ Ibid, ii. 41, 5.

of the joint-family system (i. 114, 6). They were never weary of relatives (ii. 23, 4). In other respects their conception of a home approached that of the English—"a pleasant abode,"—"a well-dressed wife,"—"an irreproachable and beloved wife," "who ornaments the chamber of sacrifice," and "adorns a dwelling," and a "draught of wine." Husband and wife were both rulers of the house ; and no doubt there subsisted concord in the family (A. V. iii. 30). This trait in their domestic character illustrates the happiness of their family life. Although they rejoiced more at the birth of sons (i. 105, 3), who were in all cases inheritors of ancestral wealth (i. 73, 9); yet they showed tender affections for daughters. They used to hold social meetings (A. V. vii. 12) ; and were also disposed to profit by the healthy influences of the company of men possessing cultivated minds (A. V. vii. 12). The unmarried daughters had a claim upon their father, brother, or other male relatives for subsistence (ii. 17, 7). And even daughters had claims to a share of the paternal property (ii. 124, 7). Women were active in their occupations ; and for them there was needle-work.* The social position of women was considerably higher than it is in modern times. They are spoken of kindly and pleasantly, as "an ornament in a dwelling" (i. 66, 3). They could converse with their husbands on equal terms, and go together and attend the sacrifices. They were also quite at liberty to walk and ride abroad (ii. 166, 3) ; and were, without any reserve, present at public feasts and games. Lovely maidens appeared in a procession ; and grown up un-

* Rig-veda, i. 292.

married daughters remained without reproach in their fathers'
houses. Our ancestors cultivated the laws of morality and
civil polity to a great extent. Their social instinct was
as old as the religions. The ties of blood were most scrupulously respected; and the extent to which matrimony
among blood-relations could not be allowed was interdicted.
They had a marriage ceremonial;[*] but it is exceedingly difficult to determine in what manner the nuptial ceremonies were performed; and what rules were
observed at such ceremonies. They had also wedding
apparel, for there is mention made of the bride's garment
(x. 85, 3, 34). On the occasion of the nuptial ceremonies,
a wish was expressed, as a rule, in the bride's favor that
she may be a queen over her father-in-law, her mother-in-
law, her husband's sister, and his brothers (x. 85, 46). The
priests gave spiritual instructions to the grown up brides as
they parted with their parents (x. 85, 15). The maidens
decorated themselves with unguents to go to their bride-
grooms (iii. 58, 9). Early marriage by no means formed
a rule; and the women enjoyed a freedom of choice in the
selection of their husbands.[†] Remarriage of widows was
not prohibited;[‡] and mention is even made of the marriage of a widow with her deceased husband's brother.[§]
It is to be stated, however, that there is no mention of
Sûdras as a class with which Brahmans intermarried. Although intermarriages between these two castes were dis-

---

[*] Rig-veda, x. 109: see also Weber's Indische Studien, v. p. 177ff.

[†] Ibid. x. 27, 11. 72; see also Taittiríya-Brâhmana. iii 4. 2. 7.

[‡] Atharva-veda. ix. 5, 27; see also Taittiríya-A'ranyaka, ci. I, 14.

[§] Rig-veda, x. 40, 2.

approved, yet we can hardly believe that they were
ever prohibited.[*] Polygamy was to a certain extent
tolerated;[†] though monogamy was the rule.[‡] There are
also references made to conjugal infidelity.[§] There were
even traces of the vices of civilization; for we read in the
Veda of common women (ii. 167, 4), of secret births (ii.
29, 1), of gambling and intoxication (v. 86, 6), and of
thieves (i. 42, 3). Prof. Weber advances some astounding
proofs of the little confidence entertained in ancient times
by the Indo-Aryans in the chastity of their women.[‖] Notwithstanding all this women were held by the authors of
the Brâhmanas in high estimation; but still there are other
places in which they are spoken of disparagingly.[**] Adul-
tery was no uncommon occurrence;[††] and it is stated
that the wife of the person offering prayers to Varuna,
must have one or more paramours.[‡‡]

Rice, barley, millet, and other kinds of grain, milk (ii.
137, 1), honey (ii. 139, 5), herbs (i. 90, 6), curd (ii. 137, 2),
ripe fruits, butter and cheese (ii. 134, 6) were their usual
meal. In the Rig-veda distinct references are made to barley
(yava);[§§] and mention of rice (vrîhi), beans (mâsha), and tila
is made in the Atharvan.[‖‖] Parched corn. (dhân),[(o)] boiled

[*] Vâjasaneyi-Samhitâ, 27, 30.
[†] Rig-veda, i. 62, 11, i. 77, 1; i. 105, 6; vii. 55, 3.
[‡] Ibid. i. 105, 3, i. 124, 7.
[§] Ibid. i. 147, 1; ix. 67, 107; x. 34, 4, x. 67, 6
[‖] Nirukta-Sûtra, iii. 4; see also Satapatha-Brâhmana, i. 2, 1, 10.
[**] Taittirîya-Samhitâ, vi. 5, 8, 2
[††] Taittirîya-Samhitâ, v. 6, 8, 3
[‡‡] Satapatha-Brâhmana ii 5, 2, 20.
[§§] Rig-veda, i. 23, 15; i. 66, 3; i. 117, 21 etc.   [‖‖] vi. 140, 2.
[(o)] Ibid. i. 16, 2; iii. 35, 3; iii. 52, 5; vi. 29, 4.

rice (odana), cakes (apûpa), and meal prepared with curd
or butter are mentioned.[o] Barley cakes mixed with milk
(v. 2, 3), boiled milk and boiled barley are alluded to
(li. 187, 9). We also read of vegetable cakes of fried meal
(ii. 187, 10). Fruit (phala) is referred to.[†] Bulls, rams,
and buffaloes formed a portion of their food.[‡] They were
also beef eaters.[§] It is true, that there was a time when
bovine meat was actually deemed a delightful food, a
token of generous hospitality in honor of a respected guest
or goghna.[‖] The slaughter of a cow on the arrival of a
distinguished guest was invariably practised in India. This
custom was so widely prevalent that goghna or "cow-
killer" came to pass as a term for such a guest. Even Pânini
has given the etymology of "cow-killer" in the sense of a
guest (iii. 4, 73). But it appears that the cow and one
of its products (gomûtra) came to be regarded as sacred
in the days of Patanjali, whose date has been fixed in the
middle of the 2nd century B. C. Bovine meat was also
considered as an essential accompaniment in the journey
from this to the future world; so much so that a cow was
in all cases burnt with the dead.

Cooking is described;[oo] and in preparing flesh meat,
part was boiled in a cauldron, part was roasted on spits, and

o Rig-veda II. 53, 7; vi. 57, 2; see also Atharva-veda, xi. 3, 22 & 42.
† Ibid, II. 45, 4.
‡ Ibid, I. 164, 43; v. 29, 7; viii. 12, 8; viii. 66, 10; x. 27, 2.
§ Wilson's Rig-veda, I. p. 105; iii. pp. 163, 270, 416 & 452.
‖ Asiatic Researches, vii. p. 288.
oo Rig-veda, ii. 117; Atharva-veda, vi. 123, 4.

part was made into balls. There were vessels to distribute
the broth ; dishes with covers, and skewers and knives
(ii. 162, 13). The queens and wives assisted in cooking and
preparing the every day meal and the banquet. There were
different kinds of earthen cooking pots (kapálas). We read
of kalsas or jar ; and of kilns or furnaces for the baking of
such vessels. And frequent mention is made of "potters,"
and of "potters' wheel." The material which was used
in the manufacture of domestic vessels was not only clay,
but also wood and leather, and even metals. They had "gold-
en cups," plates of gohl, silver, brass, and magnetic iron ;
earthen vessels (v. 104, 81), wooden vessels and cups (ii,
175, 3 ; iv. 44, 5), leather skins for water, leather bottles
and vessels (iii. 45, 1-3).

Wine was in use.* Sellers of wine are mentioned.†
Our ancestors were greatly addicted to the drinking of
spirits ; and indulged excessively both in soma and other
strong drinks. Wines or spirits were publicly sold in shops
for the general use of the community. In the Rig-veda a
hymn occurs which shows beyond all doubt that wine was
kept in leather bottles,‡ and sold without any reserve to
all comers. The Taittiríya-Bráhmana contains mantras
which speak of the preparation of the liquor ; but no information is available as to how the distillation was effected.

Our ancestors made considerable progress in their
dress. But no information is available regarding its form
and shape. It is possible that the mass of the popu-

* Rig-veda, i. 116, 7 ; vii. 86, 6 ; x. 107, 9.
† Ibid, vii. 21, 14.
‡ Ibid, x. 107, 1a.

lation wore scarfs or plaidlike articles.* The *Rig-veda* contains many texts which show that they were perfectly familiar with the art of weaving. We read of "a woman weaving a garment" (ii. 34, 4), of "female weavers," (ii. 3, 6), of the warp and the woof (vi. 9. 1), of "putting on becoming attire," of "a well-attired female," of "a well-dressed woman," (iv. 80, 6), of "elegant garments" (iii. 3, 2), and of also "elegant well-made garments (x. 107, 9 ; v. 29, 15), as fit for honorary presents. In the Yajus and the Sáman there are many allusions to clothing ; and in the former even "gold cloth" or "brocade" is mentioned.† Furs, skins, cotton, and wool (iii. 3, 4) were the only materials of which clothing was made ; and even various colors were used in dyeing textile fabrics. It appears that white clothes were especially prized (iii. 39, 2). Silk is nowhere mentioned in the Veda ; but Pánini mentions it.‡ Mention of the needle and sewing has been met with ; and there can be no doubt that our ancestors were familiar with dresses made with the aid of scissors§ and needle (ii. 32, 4). They wore turbans ; and turban or head-dress under the name of *ushnísha* is mentioned in the Atharva-veda (xv. 2, 1.)‖ Female modesty required the covering of the body down to the ankles ; and the breasts were never to be exposed. Women always wore a sheet and kanchuka

---

* Mitra's Antiquities of Orissa, I. p. 91.
† Taittiríya-Bráhmana, ii. 475.
‡ ____ i. iv. 3, 42.
§ Rig-veda, viii. 4. 16
‖ Muir's Sanskrit Texts, v. 162

over their clothes; and moved about with shoes or pattens on.[*]

The Indo-Aryans, as a rule, never cultivated the beard;
and even in those early times razor (v. 4, 16) and barber
were in every day requisition.[†] Allusions to shaving are also made.[‡] Boots, shoes and pattens were also in fashion in
those days. The material of which these were made was
bovine leather. Pânini gives words for boots; and
according to Sâmvatya as cited by A'svalâyana (iv. 9, 24),
the hide of the sacrificial cattle was even used as material
for shoes, and for other household articles. They had
umbrellas.[§] The ladies had an inordinate fondness for
ornaments and for decoration of the different parts of the
body (l. 85, 1). They also decorated themselves with garlands
(iii. 58, 6); and even some embellished themselves with
ornaments (l. 85, 8). We read of "golden ornaments" (l.
85, 4), of "golden collars," "bracelets" (iv. 53, 4), and
"fingerrings," of "an adorable uniform necklace" (ii. 33,
10), of "golden earrings," golden neck-chains, anklets,
and of "jewel necklace" (li. 122, 14). There is mention
made of pearls (x. 68, 11), and golden thread (iv. 54, 11).
In the Brâhmana of the Yajur-veda jewellery is said to
be strung in gold.[‖] Whether looking glasses formed
part of the toilet is very doubtful. They had musical in-
struments of shells and reeds; and there is mention made

* Bühler's A'parastamba, p. 14.
† Rig-veda, i. 92, 4; x. 142, 4.
‡ Rig-veda, x. 142, 4.
§ Pânini, vi. 4, 97.
‖ Taittiriya-Brâhmana, iii. 865.

of a harp with a hundred strings (i. 85, 10), and of melo-
dious lutes (ii. 34, 13). Dancers afforded them entertainment;e and for their amusement they had also puppets
(iii. 32, 23) and stage exhibitions.†

They had carriages and war chariots (iv. 42, 5) drawn
by horses; and bullock carts and waggons (i. 30, 15). The
carriages were made of wood and mounted on brazen
wheels; and had iron reins and pillars. These carriages
had seats‡ and awnings§ and they were "easy going"
(i. 13, 4), and sometimes "inlaid with gold." There were
chariots, spacious and richly ornamented with three metals,
gold, silver and copper; and fitted with golden trappings.
We also read of "three columned triangular car" (i. 47, 2),
of "golden three shafted chariots," of "golden wheels
covered with iron weapons," and of "arming the wheels."
In the Rig-veda "three benches as fixtures in each car
and the space sufficient for several persons and some goods"
are repeatedly mentioned (ii. 183, 1). They had also kasá
or whips (i. 22, 3).

Gold, silver, copper and iron were known and worked.
And they appear to have been the first to discover how to
turn iron into steel. They used golden mail, raiment and
helmet,∥ the "coat of mail" (i. 54, 3), "golden breast-
plates" (iv. 53, 4), "cuirasses of leather" (v. 5, 38), "cotton-
quilted cuirass," "golden cuirass" (iv. 54, 11), "iron mail

• Rig-veda, i. 92, 4.
† Ibid, iii. 155.
‡ Ibid, i. 175; i. 44, 2.
§ Ibid, i. 94.
∥ Ibid, i. 25, 10, 13, v. 7, 25.

and armour." The Rig-veda notices banners (i. 103, 11); and the war-cry is also alluded to (i. 87, 3). The conch-shell in battle is mentioned (i. 112, 1). The drum* was the instrument for marshalling troops or giving orders to them. The martial wind instrument is also mentioned.† The army consisted of both foot soldiers (A. V. vii. 62, 1) and mounted troops. We read of "people arrayed in martial order" (v. 79, 3); and of the commander of the whole host (i. 33, 3). There were also messengers of war (iv. 83, 3). Warriors burnished their weapons (i. 92, 1); and they gained booty from their foes in battles (i. 73, 5). We read of arrows furnished with feathers, the horns of the deer forming their points (v. 73, 11). But arrows were generally made of the sara reed with a blade of iron and besmeared with poison (i. 117, 16). Their weapons and implements were swords, spears, lances, helmets, javelins, war-missiles, discuses, clubs, bucklers, bows, quivers, arrows, shafts, axes, razors, scissors, knives, hatchets, and hooks; and those that were made of metal were sharpened on grindstones (ii. 39, 7).

Religion moulded Indian life, and all its social and political institutions. Even investigations in the various departments of knowledge are traceable to religion. Astronomical observations were first carried on simply with a view to fix the right time for the performance of the sacrifices; and the earliest beginnings of geometrical and mathematical investigations among them arose also from certain sacrificial requirements. The laws of phonetics were cultivated because

* Rig-veda, i. 23, 5, vi. 47, 39 31
† Ibid, i. 117, 21

it was a grave offence to the gods to pronounce wrongly a single letter of the sacrificial formulas; grammar and etymology were studied simply for the right understanding of the holy scriptures. And philosophy and theology have ever been closely connected.

They counted beyond a hundred.[*] The Sulva-sûtras of Baudhâyana and of Âpastamba, and the Sulva-parisisht's of Kâtyâyana contain a number of interesting rules for the construction of the various altars, which could not be done without some amount of geometrical knowledge. The property of the right-angled triangle was known to them. They also tried to express the relation between the diagonal and the side of a square, and arrived at a very close approximation. But the most interesting attempt they made in the cultivation of geometrical operations was that of squaring the circle.

The mention of the "star-gazers,"[†] of the "calculator,"[‡] of "observers of the stars," and "the science of astronomy,"[§] warrants us to conclude that astronomical science was then actively cultivated. The quinquennial cycle[¶] as well as a ennennial cycle[**] was known to them; and the division of the year was made into twelve (or 13, i. e., the intercalary month[††]) months consisting of 360 days, and each day hav-

* White Yajur-veda, xvi.
† Ibid, v. 10.
‡ Ibid, v. 20.
§ Weber's History of Indian Literature, p. 38.
¶ White Yajur-veda, v. 15; xxvii. 45; see also the Rig-veda, iii. 55, [10]; i. 25, 8.
** Taittirîya-Brâhmana, iii. 10, 4, 1
†† Rig-veda, i, 2.

ing 30 muhûrtas. The moon was to them the measurer of
time ; and there is apparently an expression of an astronomical fact that she shines only through reflecting the light of
the sun. They knew that "the sun does never set nor rise."[*]
A close observation of the moon's progress, and of the
appearance of the group of stars near which she passed, was
already made. They had also the conception of the use of
the lunar and solar years ; and of the method of adjusting
them with reference to each other.[†] And they determined the cardinal points of the horizon (i. 31, 14) ; and cal-
culated the eclipses.[‡] It was also known to them that
the earth turns regularly round the sun, whence it derives
light and heat.[§] They also divided the year into seasons.[|]
It is an interesting fact that they had some knowledge
even of the laws of attraction ;[**] and it is not improbable
that the law of gravitation may have been one of those
known to them.

We read of the constellations ;[††] and the Lunar Mansions
(the Lunar Zodiac) comprise a division of the circle
of the heavens into 27 equal parts of 13° 20' to each part.
It is to be understood that this division could not have
been made without an instrument. Our ancestors must
have possessed a knowledge of the use of appropriate appara-
tus like the armillary sphere to explain the lunar zodiac,

* Roug's Aitareya-Brahmana, ii. p. 242.
† Rig-veda, i. 25, 8.
‡ Ibid, iv 3, 12.
§ Yajur-veda, 22. 22.
| Rig-veda, i. 95, 2.
** Ibid, ii. 86-19.
†† Ibid, i. 50, 2.

and to illustrate its use. The division of the heavens into twenty-seven Nakshatras, a division which is the soul of the sacred calendar, and according to which all the Vaidik sacrifices were performed,[*] is said not to have been indigenous in India, but borrowed from without. M. Biot published several articles in the Journal des Savans, in which he tried to prove the Chinese origin of the Indian Nakshatras. He maintained that the number of the Nakshatras was originally 28, and afterwards reduced to 27. There occurs one allusion to these Nakshatras in the Veda;[†] and the 27 divisions with their asterisms and presiding deities are spoken of in the Brâhmanas. But notwithstanding these facts it has been urged that the division of the heavens into 27 Nakshatras was borrowed from China. The originality of the Veda is certainly destroyed, in case it is proved that even at that early age a foreign civilization exercised influence upon the growth of the Indian mind. M. Biot supported his favorite propositions with so much learning and skill that so ingenious a scholar as Prof. Lassen took his side, and admitted the introduction of the Chinese Sieu into northern India before the 14th century B. C.[‡] According to M. Biot's own statement the number of the Chinese Sieu was only 24, and was not raised to 28 till the year 1100 B. C. Astronomy, at least that portion of it, which bears relation to the Nakshatras, or the twenty-seven lunar mansions of the Indu-Aryans, is closely connected with the Vaidik worship.

The Vaidik sacrifices could not have been in any case performed without a knowledge of the lunar mansions. The

---

[*] Rig-veda, x. 85, 2.　　　[†] Haug's Aitareya-Brâhmana, I. pp. 42 sq.
[‡] Indian Antiquities, p. 747.

Indian names of the months were derived from the names of the constellations; and the names of the constellations again were derived, for the most part, from the names of ancient Vaidik deities.[*] The exact time of the lunar festivals is fixed with such close accuracy, that the Indo-Aryans, at the time when those public sacrifices were common, must have been, in a high degree, proficient in astronomy. The growth of astronomical knowledge in India, is closely connected with the intellectual and especially the religious history of that country. The original division of the year into lunar months must have taken effect prior to the first separation of the great Aryan family. If we find the same names of the months in Sanskrit and Chinese; and if these names the Chinese Dictionary cannot explain, surely the conclusion must be that they were borrowed by the Chinese from the Indo-Aryans, and not by the Indo-Aryans from the Chinese. The three winter months are designated in Chinese as Tchoua, Mekou, and Phalkoun; and these names correspond with the three Indian months Pausha, Mágha, and Phálguna. These Indian months received their names from the corresponding Nakshatras Pushyá, Maghá, and Phalguni. Shall we infer, then, that the Indo-Aryans borrowed the idea of the lunar Nakshatras from the Chinese, or that the Chinese borrowed them from the Indo-Aryans? The Nakshatras were indeed suggested to the Indo-Aryans by the moon's sidereal revolation; and their number was originally 27 and not 28. The Sieu were originally 24 in number; and they were afterwards raised to 28. It must be observed here that there is no

* Whitney's Súrya-Siddhánta, p. 202.

trace to be found of a like change in India. The *minstrel*
of the Arabians were also directly derived from India.
The Chinese system of *Sieu* differs from the Indian system
of Nakshatras both in its structure and its object. The
object of the Nakshatra system was to mark the progress
of the sun, the moon, and the planets through the heavens.
This Nakshatra system had from the beginning a strictly
scientific structure and application. The relation of the
Chinese *Sieu* to the Nakshatra, is altogether out of the
question. The *Sieu* throughout are but single stars;[*] while
the *Tárás* are clusters of stars. The attempt to identify
the Chinese *Sieu* with the Indian Nakshatra, or 27 lunar
mansions, is decidedly futile.

Another proof of the social progress of the Indo-Aryans is
derived from their knowledge of herbs and mode of medical
treatment. There is mention made of medicaments for the ail-
ments of our bodies (v. 74, 3): and a hymnist prays to Rudra
saying "Invigorate our sons by thy medical plants" (ii. 33,
4). "Ambrosia," says a son of Kanva, "is in the waters."
"All medicaments are in the waters" (i. 23, 20), thus anti-
cipating in so remote antiquity the hydropathic doctrine
of the present century. They had the knowledge of the
three humours of the body, i. e., wind, bile, and phlegm
(i. 34, 6) ; and of the hygienic properties of water, air,
and vegetables. Agni is said to be the remover of diseases. The Asvins are called physicians of the gods ; and
they are said to have given sight to Kanva.[†] Soma is
also supposed to preside over medicinal herbs. Anatomi-

* Whitney's Surya-Siddhanta, p. 207.
† Rig-veda, i. 117.

cal observations were then simply made by dissecting the
victims at the sacrifices. At any rate animal anatomy
was perfectly understood, as each of the different parts of
the body had its own well-defined name.* There is ample
evidence of the practice of medicine in those early days;
and we read of a "doctor who cures a patient."

* Weber's History of Indian Literature, p. 32.

CHAPTER II.

Vaidik Theogony and Mythology—Abstract Conceptions of the Deity—Cosmogony—Vaidik Doctrine of a Future Life—Priesthood and Vaidik Ceremonials of Worship.

THERE is a faculty of faith in man, a power independent of sense and reason, and the primordial source of any religion, which enables him to apprehend the Infinite. In the hymns we hear in unmistakable language the lispings of infancy, the groanings of struggling spirits for something that is neither conceivable or attainable. And in such mental struggles they formed various conceptions of the deity ; and as the case may be, they also made no apparent distinction between the concrete and the abstract, nor between the material and the spiritual. In the first stage of thought when the mind had not risen to the conception of the unity of God, it was but natural that the principal powers of nature should at first draw the attention of man ; and thus the sun, the moon and other bright objects would be worshipped and adored as they appeared to possess unbounded powers ; and that the different domains of nature should be allotted to different gods, each of whom presided over his own province. But in the *Rig-veda*

such departments are not clearly defined ; and we thus
see that one domain was presided over by more than
one deity.* The flaming orb of the mighty brilliant
sun, thunderstorm, flashing lightnings, rolling thunders,
furious blasts, rain, mists, and hail made a tremendous
impression upon the desponding minds of our ancestors.
The mind of man when so simple and childlike begins
to reflect upon the powerful and unintelligible forces
of nature, and being bewildered in its own ignorance,
in awe bows down and offers sacrifices to them. It represents them sometimes as benevolent, and sometimes as
terrible ; and ascribes to them the very same character
which it observes in daily life. Such was the natural
working of the minds of our ancestors in the childhood
of their faith. The birth of certain gods is even conceived ; and such birth can have no other than a physical meaning.† But the general absence of anthro-
pomorphism from the Vedik notions of divine beings is
conspicuous.‡ The real theogony of the Veda is not the

---

* Muir's Original Sanskrit Texts, v. p. 5.

† Müller's Chips from a German Workshop, i. p. 35.

‡ "The Vedas hold out precautions against framing a Deity after
human imagination, and recommend mankind to direct all researches
towards the surrounding objects, viewed, either collectively or individually,
bearing in mind their regular, wise, and wonderful combinations and
arrangements." —Introduction to the Abridgment of the Vedanta by Raja
Rammohan Roy, p. vii. Max Müller, in his Chips from a German Workshop, i. p. 38, says, "The religion of the Veda knows of no idols. The
worship of idols in India is a secondary formation, a later degradation of
the more primitive worship of ideal gods." Dr. Bollensen, in the Journal
of the German Oriental Society, xxii. pp. 587ff., on the other hand, contends
against this opinion. When we take into consideration the fact that the

property of the Indo-Aryans alone ; but the joint-property
of the whole Aryan race. The mythology of the Rig-veda
is sometimes very marked and distinct, and sometimes
very indistinct and hazy. But, no doubt, there is more
distinct mythology in the ninth and tenth books than in the
first eight books of the Veda. The mythology of one
Rishi is not necessarily the mythology of others ; and as
there are many Rishis, so there are many mythologies.
Max Müller has attempted to explain the Vaidik mythology
by propounding the solar theory ; and Kuhn the meteoro-
logical theory. According to the former the Aryans, as
they were highly imaginative, gave various names to the
same object ; but they soon forgot the importance or
rather the import of the original name, and consequently
mythology arose. The origin of almost all mythological
legends is solely attributable to the naive ascription of
human agency to other beings and also to animate thing s,
and consequently to their ultimate individualisation. However it was the first stage in the growth of Vaidik mythology ; but language was never at rest to spin it. It has
been very appropriately said that mythology was the bane
of the ancient world, a disease of language.[*] It is never-

ancestors were of a deep poetical temperament and of a delicate imaginative
nature, it appears very probable that the gods received a variety of ideal or
human forms and epithets. Thus they were invoked to discharge the
functions which the poetical feeling of their worshippers attributed to
them. Hence when we read of such epithets as *vripana* (Rig-veda, III. 1, 5)
&c., and of such expressions as *rūpa, rupra*, and *mandris*, we are to understand them as used only in a metaphorical sense. See on this subject
Prof. Williams' Indian Wisdom, p. 15.

* Müller's Lectures on the Science of Language, i. p. 11.

theless history changed into fable ; which is not without peculiar charms and which is also full of interesting problems that supply ample materials for the history of Aryan thought. And it is at the same time most valuable to the student of history not only in a philological, but also a philosophical, and more especially a psychological point of view.

Yáska, following the ancient expounders who preceded him, has reduced the number of the gods to three, viz., Agni whose place is on the earth ; Váyu, or Indra, whose place is in the atmosphere ; and Súrya whose place is in the sky.[*] Besides this triple classification the gods are sometimes said to be thirty-three in number ;[†] and sometimes as being much more numerous, i. e., three hundred, three thousand and thirty-nine.[‡] They are again divided into great and small, young and old.[§] But this distinction is denied in another passage ;[||] and though frequently described as immortal,[**] they are never spoken of as self-existent beings.

Dyaus, or the Greek Zeus, and Prithivi are invoked to attend religious rites ; and to grant a variety of boons. They are described as possessing physical, moral and spiritual characteristics. They are jointly called parents ;

[*] Nirukta, vii. 5., and compare Rig-veda, x 119, 1.

[†] Rig-veda, i. 34, 11 ; i. 45, 2 ; i 139, 11 ; viii. 35, 1 ; viii. 30, 9 ; viii. 35, 3 ; ix. 92, 4 ; and compare Satapatha-Bráhmana, iv. 5, 7, 2.

[‡] Rig-veda, iii. 9, 9.

[§] Ibid, i. 27, 13.

[||] Ibid, viii. 30, 1.

[**] Ibid, i. 24, 1 ; i. 72, 2, 10 ; i. 139, 3, iii. 21, 1 ; iv. 12, 1 ; x. 13, 1 : x. 68, 9.

but elsewhere the Heavens is singly called father and the
Earth mother. They are the parents of not only men but
of the gods also. They are said to be the creators and sus-
tainers of all things; but passages are not wholly wanting
where they are spoken of as themselves created. Though
Indra is said to be their creator; yet they are also spoken
of as created by Soma, Púshan, Dhátri and Hiranyagarbha.
They are also said to have received their shape from
Tvashtri, and to have sprung from the head and feet of
Purusha; and to be supported by Mitra, Savitri, Varuna,
Indra, Soma and Hiranyagarbha.

Aditi is the only goddess spoken* of by name in the
Rig-veda. What is not Diti is Aditi. She is styled the
goddess or the divine; and is the source and supporter of
all things, and represents the whole nature. She is
supplicated for different blessings, and for forgiveness of
sins. She is said to be the mother of Varuna and of other
gods;* and her gifts are pure and celestial. She, as the
great power, wields the forces of the universe, and controls men by moral laws. In the Sáma-veda Aditi is
represented with her sons and brothers. The sons are
styled A'dityas; and they are Mitra, Aryaman, Bhaga,
Varuna, Daksha and Ansa.† But in some places they are
stated to be seven, in others eight in number, though their
names are not given there. They are described as sleep-
less, many-eyed, vast, strong, bright, holy, pure, golden,
sinless, blameless. They are far-observing; and all things

---

* M. Ad. Regnier, Étude sur l'idiome des Vedas, p. 28.

† Rig-veda, ii. 27. 1.

are near to them. They see good and evil in men's
hearts, and punish sin.

Mitra is frequently associated with Varuna. Varuna,
however, is sometimes separately celebrated; Mitra but
seldom. Mitra etymologically signifying *measurer*, was
originally the name of the day; and Varuna etymologically
signifying *coverer*, was originally the name of the night.
Mitra and Varuna are the most important from the identification of the former with the Mithra of the Zend-
Avesta;[*] and of the latter with the Uranos of the
Greeks. Varuna occupies a rather more prominent place
in the hymns; he presides over light, and it is said in
one passage that the constellations are his holy acts, and
that the moon moves by his command. He is called the
source of light; he grants wealth, averts evil, and protects
cattle. In another passage, he is said to abide in the
ocean, and to be acquainted with the course of ships. He
is also said to know the flight of birds in the sky, and the
regular succession of months. His character does not,
however, appear to have been the same throughout the
whole period represented by the Vaidik hymns. He is
the sovereign of his own abode; and a king both of the gods
and of men often surrounded by his messengers. He is
mighty, fixed in purpose, far-sighted and visible to his
worshippers. To him are attributed the grandest cosmical

* Herodotus confounds Mitra with Mylitta; but the important thing
to be observed is, that Mitra was a Persian god. There are evidently many
passages in the Vend-idad which prove that among the ancient Persians
Mithra was sometimes represented as the Sun. But the modern Pârsis
understand by it Meher Ized, in contradistinction to Khorshéd, the Sun.

functions. He is said to have created the Heaven and the
Earth ; and to uphold, and rule over them. He possesses high
moral character more than any other gods. His laws are
fixed and unimpeachable ; and he controls the destinies of men. He is besought to drive away evil, to give
deliverance from sin, and to prolong life. The same attributes and functions are also ascribed to Mitra. Varuna
was an older god than Indra ; and the homage originally
paid to the former was gradually transferred to the
latter. The Varuna-worship declined, and the Indra-worship
superseded it. This was the result of the gradual change
which marked the Indo-Aryan religion. The anteriority of
Varuna to Indra is borne out by the coincidence of his
name with the Uranos of the Greek mythology ; while all
attempts at the identification of Indra with any other
character of the same mythology are out of the question.

Indra was human ; he is reputed as the destroyer
of Vritra, an Asura or Assyrian. His original name
was Ind. He was deified for his exploits. He is
described as being born ; and as having both parents.
He is also said to have been produced by the gods ; and
to have sprung from the mouth of Purusha. He is a twin
brother of Agni. The highest divine attributes and functions are attributed to him. He is spoken of in some places
as having physical superiority ; and in others as having no
spiritual elevation or moral grandeur ; though there are
various other texts in which he is found to be invested
with ethical character. He is besought by men like a
father, and for temporal blessings ; and even faith in him
is enjoined. He is represented as heroic, strong, martial,

ancient, youthful, undecaying and wielding the thunderbolt. He is golden ; and can assume any shape at will.
His wife is alluded to ; and his intimate relation with his
worshippers is spoken of. He is the destroyer of enemies ;
and he conquered heaven by austerity.

Vâyu, the blower, is frequently found in conjunction with
Indra ; and does not seem to occupy a very prominent place
in the Ŗig-veda. He is the son-in-law of Twashtri ; and is
spoken of as beautiful in form. Pûshan nourished the growth
of crops. He is the protector on a journey, particularly of
robbers ; and he is said to be the divinity presiding over
the earth. He is connected with the marriage ceremonial (x. 85, 26 and 37); and is supplicated to take the
bride's hand and lead her away, and to bless her in her
conjugal relation. Rudra literally means one who cries ;
and in process of time he became the god of thunder.
The character of Rudra is identical with that of Pûshan.
He is the source of fertility, and the giver of happiness ;
and he is said to preside over medicinal plants, and is invoked for the removal of diseases. He is represented as the
lord of evil spirits. He was originally an object of worship
with the aborigines ; and such worship was gradually
adopted by the Indo-Aryans. The Maruts, the pounders, or
Rudras are the sons of Rudra and Priśni. They are very
commonly represented as the attendants of Indra, and as the
children of the ocean. They are spoken of as golden-foot-
ed ; and they are said to worship Indra. The Maruts were
the leaders of hunters ; but in course of time they seem
to have lost their anthropopathic character. The invocations of the Viśve-devâh or the All-gods as they are called,

represent a later phase of thought than the invocations of each individual deity singly. They are nine in number, such as Indra, Agni, Mitra, Varuna and the rest. They are besought as preservers of men, and as bestowers of rewards.

Agni (is identical with the Latin Ignis) is indeed called the lowest of the gods, but notwithstanding this he is greatly revered. He is invoked at all sacrifices; and as he is the sacrificial fire, he is the servant of both men and of the gods, carrying the invocations and the offerings of the former to the latter; he invites the gods to the ceremonies; and performs them in behalf of the lord of the house. Represented as a divinity, his is immortality, his is never-failing youth, invested with infinite power and glory. He is the grantor of life, health, food, wealth and cattle. He is the source of effulgent light, and the destroyer of all things. He is golden-haired and an emblem of purity. He is known under various appellations; and many deities inferior to him are purely his manifestations. He is identified with Vishnu, Varuna, Mitra, Indra, Aryaman, Yama, Ansa, Tvashtri, Rudra, Pushan, Savitri, Bhaga, Aditi, Hotri, Bharati, Ila, Saraswati, and with the eternal Vedhas; and the functions and attributes of other deities are often ascribed to him. He is the son of the Heaven and the Earth; and elsewhere he is said to have been generated by the gods, and to have been brought from the sky by Matarisvan. His production is also attributed to the waters. He again is the father of the gods; and is regarded as having a triple existence. He knows the races of the gods and of men. He is the protector, friend, and leader of the people. He is the divine king, and is as strong as Indra; and is worshipped by Varuna, Mitra, the Maruts, and all the three thousand, three hundred and thirty-nine gods.

Súrya, or the Greek Helios, and Savitri are exact personifications of the sun; and under these two different epithets the sun is chiefly represented in the hymns. Súrya is spoken of as an A'ditya; and occupies in the Vaidik worship a place not so prominent as could be naturally anticipated from the magnificence and splendour of that luminous body. He is said to be god-born, and to have been generated by Indra, Agni, Soma, Mitra, and Varuna. He is the divine leader or the priest of the gods. Like Agni and Indra, he is the source of light, and the greater of temporal blessings. He is all-seeing; and he beholds the good and bad deeds of the mortals. He is said to be the healer of leprosy. Only three satras in the first book of the Rig-veda are addressed to him; and these "convey no very strikingly expressive acknowledgment of his supremacy." Although the Sun-worship was not prominent, the Indo-Aryans loved light and even warmth, and the sun or the "ray diffuser." The expressions contained in the hymns relating to this deity exhibit a careful and loving observation of Nature. He is spoken of as coming "from a distance," and "removing all sins;" or as the divine Sun he is supplicated to take away the "sickness of the heart," and the "yellowness of the body."

Savitri, who was originally the autumnal sun, is sometimes distinguished from Súrya: and is frequently identified with Mitra and Púshan. He is the golden deity, yellow-haired, golden-handed, and golden-tongued. He is the bestower of all desirable things; and confers blessings from the sky, from the atmosphere, and from the earth. He is said to have bestowed immortality on the gods.

The Aswins are in various texts connected with Sûrya. They are the twin sons of Vivasvat and Saranyû; and are also called the sons of the sky. They are described as young, beautiful, ancient, strong, bright, terrible, and skilful. They bestow food and wealth. They ever occupy themselves with multifarious earthly transactions, enable the worshippers to baffle their enemies, assist them in their need, and extricate them from difficulty. Their business is more earthly than heavenly. They cure the blind, the lame, the emaciated, and the sick. They are besought for different blessings; for long life, offspring, wealth, victory, destruction of enemies, and forgiveness of sins. The myth of the human Aswins has two distinct elements, one cosmical and the other human or historical; which have in course of time become blended into one. The cosmical element refers to their luminous nature; and the human element to the wonderful cures effected by them. They were probably some renowned mortals, horsemen of celebrity, who were admitted on account of their wonderful medical skill to the companionship of the gods.

Twashtri (the Vulcan) is frequently found connected with the Ribhus. He is the divine artisan, the skilful worker, and the creator of all forms. He is also versed in all magical devices. He forges the thunderbolts of Indra. He bestows long life, offspring, wealth and protection; and forms husband and wife for each other. He is supplicated to preserve the worshippers. He was also a renowned mortal; and as the skilful artisan he had been translated into the companionship of the gods.

Soma is the god who plays an important part in the sacrificial act of the Vaidik age. He is said to be divine, and the soul of sacrifice. He is the king of the gods and of men. He is the lord of creatures; and the generator of the sky and earth, of Agni, Súrya, Indra and Vishnu. He is wise, strong, agile, and thousand-eyed. He beholds all the worlds, and destroys the irreligious. He is immortal, and confers immortality on the gods and on men. He is generous as a father to a son; and is supplicated to forgive sins. In the post-Vaidik age the name Soma came to be commonly applied to the moon and its regent. Even in the Rig-veda some traces of this application seem to be discoverable.[*]

The connexion of the personified Dawn or Ushas (the Aurora of the Latins) with Súrya makes its worship a form of solar adoration. The hymns put up to her, are not wrapped up in mystic language or fantastic allegory. The invigorating influence which the dawn exercises on both the body and the mind; and the luminous and other pleasant phenomena connected with day-break, constitute the subject of some of the best portions of Vaidik poetry; and out of them the conceptions of Ushas arose. She is invoked as the affluent, as the

[*] i. 85, 8 ff.; and compare, "The transference of the name Soma to the moon, which appears in the later history of the Indian religion, is hitherto unknown: the Vedas hardly know it, nor do they seem to prepare the way for it in any manner."—Whitney's Oriental and Linguistic Studies, p. 11.

giver of food, and bringer of opulence; she is asked to lavish on the pious riches, honors, cattle, posterity, and troops of slaves; and she is praised for the numerous and various boons she bestowed on the worshippers who were liberal to her. She is the goddess imbued with an excellent intellect, is truthful, and the fulfiller of her promises. She invigorates the diligent; when she appears, bipeds and quadrupeds are in motion; the winged birds hover in the air; and men who have to earn their bread quit their homes. She rides, in a golden chariot, which is large and beautiful. The relation of Ushas to other Vaidik deities is two-fold, physical and ritual, in as much as the phenomena of the dawn are associated with the other phenomena of Nature, and as certain religious ceremonies are held at the beginning of the day. For this, she is frequently addressed as the daughter of the Heaven; and when her parents are spoken of, the commentators explain this word as signifying the Heaven and the Earth. She is farther called the daughter of the night; but, on other grounds, she is also described as having Night for her sister. Besides, she is the sister of Bhaga, the kinswoman of Varuna, and the faithful wife of Sûrya.

Parjanya or Perkunas[*] is the thundering rain-god. He appears to have been associated with Vâta, the blast, and Agni; but was decidedly distinct from Indra. He is called the son of Dyaus, and the father of the Soma plant. He is represented as the lord of all moving creatures.

---

[*] Benfey's Orient and Occident, i. p. 214.

He presides over the lightning, thunder, and rain ; and is said to impregnate the plants.

Brahmanaspati or Brihaspati is described as the offspring of the two Worlds. He appears sometimes to be identical with Indra ; but is elsewhere distinguished from Agni. He is styled the father of the gods ; and is possessed of all divine attributes. He is bright, pure, clear-voiced, opulent, and a remover of diseases. He is called a priest ; and intercedes with the gods on behalf of men. He is the protector of the pious ; and saves them from all dangers.

Trita A'ptya, Ahirbodhnya, and Aja Ekapád are minor divinities. Trita is conjoined with the Maruts, with Váta or Váyu, and Indra. He is called A'ptya ; and his abode is hidden. He bestows long life. Ahirbudhnya is the Dragon of the deep ; and resides in the atmospheric ocean. Aja Ekapád is probably a storm-god.

Sarasvati is a goddess of some importance in the Rig-veda. She is celebrated both as a river and as a deity. She was indeed primarily a river-deity. She bestows prosperity, wealth, offspring and fertility. She attends the sacrifices along with other goddesses, Bhárati, Hotrá, Varútri, Mahi, Ilá, Dhishaná. Araṇyáni is mentioned as the goddess of forest solitude. Anumati or "the moon one digit less than full," Ráká, or "the full moon," Sinívali, or "the last day before the new moon," and Kuhú or Gungú, or "the new moon," are some other goddesses represented in the hymns. Ráká is closely connected with parturition. Sraddhá is an object of adoration in the morning, at noon, and at sunset. She is the personification of an abstract idea or religious faith. She prospers the liberal worshippers of the gods, and imparts faith. Lakshmi and Sri do not occur in the hymns in the sense as they appear in the later mythology. Sri is mentioned as issuing forth from Prajápati when he was wrapped up in intense austerity. Aditi, the mother of the A'dityas, is the representative of the universe ; Diti her counterpart. Nishígrí is the mother, and Indráni the wife, of Indra. Prisni is the mother of the Maruts. Súryá is the daughter of the sun, and the spouse of the Asvins, or of Soma. Besides these goddesses a few others, such as Agnáyí, Varunáni, Rodasí, and Aramati are also celebrated in the hymns of the Rig-veda.

No reference to tangible things as objects of worship has been discovered in the old hymns. But with regard to semi-tangible and intangible objects, the case is really very different.[*] Most of the gods are merely poetical names, names denoting purely sensuous objects ; which gradually assumed a divine personality of course never thought of by the original authors. These names no doubt had originally their material meaning ; but gradually they came to be used in the spiritual sense. They again were sometimes used merely as appellatives ; and sometimes as names of gods. It is thus seen that many names were created owing to the utter helplessness of the worshippers to express their ideas of the deity. Indeed, names after names were created to express the infinity and the majesty of the divine ; and this was only suggested by the consciousness of the insufficiency of those names that had been already created and used to convey such ideas.

[*] Müller's Hibbert Lectures, p. 191.

However, every name was created with a distinct purpose; and so had a history full of useful lessons. And in fact an idea of a deity under such varying disguises evinces a great progress of thought. It is thus clear that the idea of God existed in a vague and hazy form; who was not yet defined or properly named. The names given to God gradually came to signify distinct divinities. There may be error in all those names; but the simple attempt to give a name was the greatest triumph of the adoring poets; who had a longing for God, who felt kinship between themselves and God,[*] and who invented names after names to grasp and comprehend him. A name, however, is not a mere name, not a hollow phraseology, it is not mute, but has life in it. And in such names there must have been, as it were, some presentiments of monotheism. The hymns were composed neither in the same age, nor by the same poet, nor did they originate at the same localities, nor under the same circumstances. They are the work of many Rishis and of many centuries. There could be found, therefore, neither much consistency of thought nor of idea in them. As the conceptions of the different poets could be various, so the natures of the gods must have differentiated. The same god is represented in one hymn as supreme and equal; and again in others as inferior. There are also many passages in which the attributes of infinity, omnipotence, and omnipresence are ascribed to each of the gods.[†] However, the whole nature of those

---

[*] Rig-veda., i. 11, 13; vii. 47, 8; vii. 82, 32; x. 142, 1.

[†] Rig-veda, x. 90, 1 ff; x. 121, 1 ff.

ideal and imaginary gods is still transparent; they are merely names of natural phenomena and are without being; they are the creatures of man and not his creators. Here names play with us. The consciousness that all the deities are but different names of one and the same godhead is manifest in some of the hymns of the Veda. In one hymn it is distinctly stated that the gods, though differently named and represented, are really one and the same; but men call them by different names, and the poets represent the one and the same god in different forms:—"They call him Indra, Mitra, Varuna, Agni; and (he is) the well-winged, celestial Garutmat. Sages name variously that which is but one:—they call it Agni, Yama, Mâtarisvan."[*] Savitri is the supporter of the sky and the lord of creatures.[†] Varuna is said to be the lord of all, of gods and men, of heaven and earth.[‡] Indra is also clearly conceived as the supreme god;[§] and as regards the character and functions of Tvashtri we have an approach to the idea of a supreme creator of the universe. According to the Taittiriya-Brâhmana the gods attained their divine rank by austerity.[‖] They are said to possess in an eminent degree the qualities of the Rishis; and so they are also styled Kavi, Rishi, etc.[¶] This possibly implies that the

* Rig-veda, i. 164, 46; see also Colebrooke's Essay, i. 26 (; Weber's Indische Studien, v. p. iv.

† Ibid, iv. 53, 2.

‡ Ibid, i. 25, 20; ii. 27, 10.

§ Ibid, vii. 32.

‖ Muir's Original Sanskrit Texts, iii. p. 278.

¶ Rig-veda, x. 29, 1; vi. 16, 2; vii. 6, 43; viii. 16, 7; ix. 96, 18; ix. 107, 7; x. 27, 22; x. 112, 9.

Rishis thought they possessed particular knowledge of the deities, with whom they believed they had an affinity. "Indeed, the relations between the Vaidik Aryans and their deities appear to have been of a childlike and filial character ; the evils which they suffered, they ascribed to some offence of omission or commission which had been given to a deity ; whilst the good which they received was in like manner ascribed to his kindness and favor."[*] The deities of the primitive Vaidik times represented not only the conspicuous processes of external nature ; but also the higher relations of moral and social life. The songs with which the Indo-Aryans invoked the gods clearly show that they sought them for their spiritual as well as for their material welfare. Ethical considerations are not, therefore, extraneous to these instinctive outbursts of the pious mind. The distinction between good and bad was made in a moral sense ; and law and virtue were also recognized.[†] Sin and evil, indeed, are often adverted to ; and the gods are extolled because they destroy sinners and evil-doers.[‡] Even the idea of personal sin is to be met with in the Black Yajus. "May our sins be removed" or " repented of " is the burden of several hymns in the Rik (i, 97 ; ii. 24, 5 ; ii. 83, 6 ; vii. 32, 9 ; viii. 13, 15) ; and there is only one other hymn in which the hymnist prays to be absolved not only from his own sins but also from the sins of his fathers (vii. 86). It is not so diffi-

---

* Wheeler's History of India i. p. 18

† Rig-veda, ii 29, 5 ; d 29, 1.

‡ Ibid. 1 15, 9, 11 ; b 26, 14 ; i 115, 6 ; a 27, 11 ; and see also Johnson's Oriental Religions, p. 118.

cult now to have the idea as to the writers' notion of sin or of repentance when it is an undeniable fact that they distinctly acknowledged two eternal principles of Good and Evil. The two ideas of justice and mercy are also to be met with in the hymns.[*] However, there are to be found many hymns in the Rik which depart materially from the simplicity of the conceptions here alluded to.

Our Aryan ancestors carried with them their religion and worship when they started from their primitive home, and spread themselves over the various parts of the world. Therefore, among different branches of the family there is to be found a great harmony which subsisted in their original worship and in the names of God and of the gods. Indeed, the Indo-Aryans, Greeks, Romans, Germans, Celtics at one time worshipped the same gods. Although Indo-Aryan mythology is extravagant and ridiculous, and has an icy coldness of meaning in it, yet those mythological dreams have an enduring symbolic value, and stand as data for primitive history. The Indo-Aryans early speculated largely on matters supernatural ; and their religion was an important feature of their civilisation. The Vaidik religion in all its aspects is the true expression of the view which our simple-minded but highly gifted ancestors imbued with deep religious feelings, took of the wonderful powers and phenomena of nature. And there is no doubt that it originated in the minds of single individuals, whether inspired or not inspired ; but this cannot be said of the whole

body of the people. In the hymns there is a deep
awakening of the religious sentiment, and a sense of the
divine. In all the objects of nature our ancestors beheld
either the primary causes of them, or the visible em-
blems of the invisible great cause. But once the religious faculty being roused, the human mind, which is subtle
introversive and contemplative, could never be satisfied
with the mere idea that the elements are the sole cause
of creation ; and so it must go on to spiritualise the
gigantic forms of nature by which we are surrounded ;
and as to the extent to which the beautiful conceptions
of poetic fancy are carried, religion must of necessity
become fetichism, pantheism, or polytheism. And polytheism can only be the result when each spirit is allowed
to assume a separate form, and is invested with attributes
as worthy as could be of its emblem. In the oldest portions of the hymns, there are few traces to be found of
abstract conceptions of the deity. They apparently dis-
close the primitive stage of religious belief of simple men :
who, under the influence of the most wonderful phenomena of nature, felt every where the presence and agency
of divine powers ; and who had not then risen to a clear
idea of one Supreme God. Our ancestors imagined that
each of the provinces of the universe was controlled and
regulated by each of the deities ; and this is clearly
shown by the special functions assigned to them, and by
the very names under which they are designated.

The Vedas contain no real system ; they never classify
or define the objects of worship. This was, however,
done at last by commentators, who seem to have generally

misunderstood the religion taught in them. Every object in the universe awed our earliest forefathers and
roused them from stolid wonderment to think and ponder;
and thus in the childhood of their faith they looked for the
infinite in the moon and the sun, in the sky, in the storm,
and in a flash of lightning. And so they called it at one time
wielder of thunderbolt, giver of rain, bringer of light, thun-
derer, bestower of food and life; and at last creator, preser-
ver, ruler, king, father, and god of gods. All this we see in
one great evolution of religious thought, as no concept is
possible without a name. All that we see is that they
felt the presence of God in every object they behold in
the universe; and that they tried to rise from Nature up
to Nature's God. However, it is really impossible to give
a name to the religion of the Ṛṣis. They used words
which are always extremely important, both psychologi-
cally and historically. But we cannot use them now in
their etymological meaning nor in the senses which must
have passed at one time through an historical evolution.
Faith, worship, hope and reverence for the gods—all this
was religion to them. But we cannot characterise the
ancient Vaidik religion as Henotheism or Kathenotheism;
it is impossible to give a general name for it. There are
numerous passages in the Rig-veda in many of which a
monotheistic and in many others a pantheistic tendency is
very clearly manifested. In the later stage of reflection
our ancestors very possibly made approximations to monotheistic tendencies; and those approximations could only
be weak and sporadic; and thus such a speculative
monotheism was of necessity of a forced and shadowy

character. In the hymns there are traces of human
conceptions, human aspirations, human wisdom, and
human folly. They have their material and spiritual
aspect; they are at once vaguely pantheistic, severely
monotheistic, grossly polytheistic, and coldly atheistic.
They contain but the common principle of all the four.
This prehistoric star-dust of all the systems may properly be called pantheism not in its exclusive sense. It is
not philosophical abstraction but intense realisation. The
polytheism of the Vedas like their pantheism is in the free,
plastic age. The complicated polytheism which we find
in the hymns is but the full development of polytheism of
anterior centuries. It is evident that monotheism was
never the starting point of the Vaidik system. We cannot conceive at the first stage of thought of the unity existing under the diversity; and such a conception as the
first fruit of theosophic philosophy, is decidedly of later
growth, and the result of subsequent reflection and comparison. We are therefore led to believe that monotheism
never preceded polytheism. When the human spirit is
once gifted with clear ideas of the unity of nature and
of its Author, it is not possible that it should ignore
that original cognition, and betake itself to the vagaries
of naturalism and the worship of the multifarious deities
of the proper Vaidik Olympus.

The ideas of entity and non-entity were very well familiar to the Vaidik *Rishis*.* In the 90th hymn of the tenth
book of the *Rig-veda* the unity of the godhead is recog-

* *Rig-veda*, x. 72.

nised, although in a clearly pantheistic sense. We see
elsewhere that the sun, the sky, and the earth were at one
time considered as natural objects generated by the gods;
and at another time as themselves the gods who created
all things. Some scholars have gone so far as to assert
that the idea of one God breaks through the mist of a polytheistic and an idolatrous phraseology. This is a mistake.
The human mind in its natural operation strives to reduce
all objects and events to unity and harmony, and to
trace everything to a single source; and until there
could be made a sufficient progress towards the knowledge
of the unity and harmony of this marvellous universe, it is
not possible for men to attain to a real conception of the
unity of the Godhead. Oneness of god does not however
exclude the idea of plurality of gods. There was no word
yet to express the abstract idea of an immaterial and supernatural Being. The attributes of supremacy and omnipotence ascribed to one god did by no means exclude the
admission of gods or names of gods. And it is also clear
from the hymns that the poets never thought of other gods
when they addressed their own god. But in some cases this
idea is not admissible with the worship of two in the dual as
Mitrâ-varunau, Indrâ-somau, etc., or many in one group
in the plural, as the Visve-devâs and the Maruts. The Vaidik hymns are, in one sense, both physiolatrous and polytheistic. The age when they were composed, as appears
clearly from the Brahmanas or directories for their use in the
Brahma sacrifices, was followed by a palpable deterioration
in the thought and feeling of the Indo-Aryans. At first the
polytheism was simple. "The polytheistic idea, however,

when once it had begun to work, would tend constantly
to multiply the number of divinities, as we see it has already done in the Vaidik age."[*] There never was nor
could be a pure polytheism or a pure monotheism. It is
beyond doubt, that the human mind, in proportion to its
power of observation and reflection, advances towards
monotheism. But it is to be confessed that such movement
is very slow, and often obstructed by tradition and habit.
We must not place at the commencement that which
ought to be placed at the very end. However, it is clear
that our ancestors were polytheists before their separation ;
and they could never completely forget what they once
learnt and brought with them as a heritage from their
original home. Such teaching, which again they had left
as a legacy, had acted, upon the whole, most potently on
the minds of their descendants from generation to generation ; until the proper philosophical age dawned, and the
Upanishads were composed and their doctrines had taken
ground. But the influence of such philosophical writings
has been in no way complete nor permanent ; and their
attempts towards obliteration at once from the mind, of the
polytheistic principles, were far from being successful.

The Indo-Aryans had not attained to a clear and
logical comprehension of the characteristics which they
themselves ascribed to the objects of their worship. The
conceptions of the Godhead indicated in the hymns are
of a fluctuating and undecided character. The remarkable
representations of a host of subordinate objects of worship, exhibit to us a conception of the universe by our

* Pictet's Origines Indo-Européennes, ii. pp. 706 ff.

ancestors which was mythical, sacramental, polytheistic, and even pantheistic. In the childhood of the world, the Indo-Aryans possessing simple and reflective minds solved the mysterious and difficult problem of the production of the existing universe in various ways. They entertained a great number of different conjectures with regard to cosmogony. As the case may be, they ascribed it sometimes to physical, and sometimes to spiritual powers. And as speculation gradually acquired vigour, different opinions asserted themselves, and they naturally became perplexed; and one of them asks: "What was the forest, what was the tree, out of which they fashioned heaven and earth? Inquire with your minds, ye sages, what was that on which he (Visvakarman) took his stand when supporting the world?"* Another poet asks, "Which of them two was the first, and which the last? How have they been produced? Sages, who knows?"† And as further speculations were carried on they gradually arrived at the idea of the universe having sprung out of darkness and a pre-existing chaos :‡ this notion could only have presented to them by the changes which constantly occurred before their eyes in the universe. And this

* Rig-veda, x. 81, 4; see also Taitriya-Brahmana, ii. 8, 9, 6.

† Ibid, i. 185, 1.

‡ Compare Genesis, i. 1. Here the meaning of the verb bará is rendered by "created." But it simply conveys the sense of mere fashioning or arranging; and does by no means signify an ex nihilo creation. There is also no trace of the meaning attributed to it by later scholars of a creation out of nothing. According to the Jewish commentators it does not represent so. However, this idea is altogether a modern idea; and to transfer a modern idea to the mind of Moses is simply absurd.

doctrine is found to be propounded in one of the later hymns of the *Rig-veda.*[*] In different other hymns, however, we meet with various speculations about the origin of heaven and earth. The creation of them is sometimes ascribed to Indra, and at other times to other deities, such as Soma, Púshan, Dhátri and Hiranyagarbha. And it is also said that they have received their shape from Tvashtri, and have sprung from the head and feet of Purusha; and are supported by Mitra, Varuna, Indra, Agni, Savitri and Soma. Elaborate theories of creation are not to be found in the earlier portions of the hymns;[†] and even the Rishis themselves apparently confess their ignorance of the beginning of all things.[‡]

There is a hymn in the tenth book of the *Rig-veda* of a long antecedent period, of philosophical thought in which we find the conception of a beginning of all things, and of a state, before all things were created. In the beginning there was nothing, no sky, no firmament. No space there was, no life, no time, no difference between day and night. "Darkness there was, and all at first was veiled in gloom profound, as ocean without light." There was only the deep abyss, a chaotic mass, which swallowed every thing. "That one," the poet says, "breathed, and lived; it enjoyed more than mere existence; yet its life was not dependent on any thing else, as our life depends on the air which we breathe. It breathed breathless." Max Müller says "language blushes at such expressions,

* *Rig-veda.* x. 129.
† Ibid, i. 67, 3 ; x. 82, 1
‡ Ibid, i. 164, 4 ; x. 82, 4.

but her blush is a blush of triumph." The creation is sometimes said to be the manifestation of His will; and a mere evolution of one substance. The idea of the spontaneous evolution of all things out of undeveloped matter, became the foundation of the Sânkhya philosophy. In that remote period we find that the difference between mind and matter was but imperfectly conceived.

The history of mankind clearly shows that man is essentially religious; and the belief in the unseen spiritual world has its foundation in our nature. The high-water marks of the radical elements of real religion, such as an intuition of God, a sense of human weakness and a feeling of dependence on God, a belief in a divine government of the world, a distinction between good and evil, and a hope of a better life, break forth in the Rigveda. But the earlier portions of the Rik allude very little to a future state; and even references to a future state of punishment in all the Vedas are few and far between: and again these references are very obscure. Our ancestors had not contempt for all things beneath the sun, nor had they any dislike for this existence with all its vicissitudes and miseries. So they longed for continuation of life, and death by no other cause than by old age; and also thought of this life simply as a preparation for a new existence in the world of the departed where to enjoy eternal bliss. They however had no idea of retribution after death; and it was their simple faith that the new existence would be merely a continuation of the old age though under changed conditions. There also appears a simple faith that the life in this world is not the last of man;

but after death he is to go to a place of happiness above." In a passage we read that the highest object of life is to restore that bond which links self to the eternal Self.[†] There also occurs another passage about being and non-being; which clearly shows that, that philosophical dogma was known to the Indo-Aryans at so early a period.[‡]

In the ninth and tenth mandalas of the Rig-veda there are some distinct references made to a future life. Besides these there are other texts which intimate the same belief. The consciousness of sin is the prominent characteristic of the religion of the Veda. It is said that the gods take away from man the burden of his sins.[§] The idea of faith is also found in the Rig-veda;[||] and that faith is again associated sometimes with true scepticism.[¶] In the Veda there are to be found certain passages in which

* Prof. Roth, after extracting several passages from the Rik in which a belief in immortality is clearly conveyed, says with great force,—" We have had, not without astonishment, beautiful conceptions on immortality, expressed in unadorned language with child-like conviction. If it were necessary, we might here find the most powerful weapons against the view which has lately been revived, and proclaimed as new, that Persia was the only birthplace of the idea of immortality, and that even the nations of Europe had derived it from that quarter; as if the religious spirit of every gifted race was not able to arrive at it by its own strength."—Journal of the German Oriental Society, ix. p. 687 ; Muir's Original Sanskrit Texts, v. p. 301.

† Rig-veda, x. 129, 4.

‡ Taittiriya-Brāhmaṇa, ii. p. 933 : अव्यक्तादीनि अव्यक्तानि अव्यक्तनि ।

§ Rig-veda, i. 162, 22 ; ii. 27, 6 ; iv. 12, 4 ; v. 82, 6 ; vii. 87, 7 ; vi. 93, 7 ; viii. 44, 9 ; x. 25, 3.

|| Ibid, i. 100, 3 ; i. 104, 6 ; i. 55, 5.

¶ Ibid, viii. 100, 3.

occurs not only the idea of immortality of the soul, of personal immortality, but also of personal responsibility after death. That immortality was gained by a son is mentioned in one passage of the Veda ;* and one poet prays that he may again see his father and mother after death.† It is also said that immortality is secured even by a son.‡ The gods are said to have established the eternal laws of right and wrong ; and they punish sin and reward virtue. Morality and religion were closely connected." But still the enjoyments of a future life are most probably to be understood as of a sensual kind.§ The gods themselves were regarded as subject to the influence of carnal appetites.‖ Some of the hymns attribute to the gods sentiments and passions, such as anger, revenge, and delight in sacrifices ; and represent man with all the desires and weaknesses of his nature. Immunity from taxation is held out as the greatest boon to be received in the next world.¶ A funeral hymn addressed to Agni** contains some verses which fully give the views of the writer on a future life. The pitris, or fathers of families, who have departed this life and passed to a state of blessedness are represented as objects of adoration to their descendants. The fathers are supplicated almost like gods ; worship

* Rig-veda, vii. 88. 24.
† Rig-veda, i. 24, 1 ; compare Atharva-veda, xii. 8, 27.
‡ Rig-veda, vii. 56, 24 : compare Gopatha-Brahmana, i. 1, 2.
§ Rig-veda, ix. 113, 7 ff. ; compare Atharva-veda, iv. 34, 2.
‖ Rig-veda, iii. 53, 6 ; Atharva-veda, xx. 3, 31 f.
¶ Atharva-veda, xi. 29, 2.
** Rig-veda, x. 16.

F

and oblations are offered to them ;* and they are said to
enjoy in the company of the gods, a life of eternal felici-
ty.† It is said, that there exist three heavens‡ of which
the *pitris* occupy the highest. The Vaidik doctrine of the
pitris chimes in with the Greek and Roman doctrine about
the manes. In certain passages of the *Rig-veda* the word
manas is found to be used for the soul or the animating
principle which is never annihilated after the termination
of earthly existence.§ *Atman* is also employed in several
portions of the *Rig-veda* for the living principle ; and in
some places the sun is also addressed as the soul of all
things changeable or unchangeable.‖ Some texts refer in-
distinctly to the punishment of the wicked.¶ In the Atharva-veda the adjective form of the usual word for hell
(*ndraka loka*) occurs : and that region is described as the
future abode of the illiberal.**

From the *Rig-veda* we learn that the Rishis had conceived the idea of the soul being immortal.†† There is a
prayer of Vasishtha addressed to Varuna (vii. 86) which

---

* Rig-veda. i 16. 2, 9 ; see also on the Offerings to the Pitris. Colebrooke's Essay on the Religious Ceremonies of the Hindus.—Miscellaneous
Essays, r pp 180, &c.

† Rig-veda, i 19. 1. Atharva-veda. xviii 2, 49.

‡ Atharva-veda. xviii 2 48.

§ Rig-veda. i 88, 1. Compare Atharva-veda, xviii 1, 23 . "Let thy soul
(*manas*) go to its own and hasten to the fathers." The mind (*manas*) is
regarded by the Hindu philosophers as distinct from the soul.

‖ Rig-veda, i 115, 1 ; ix. 2, 10 ; ix. 6, 9 ; ix. 85, 2

¶ Rig-veda, iv 5, 5 ; vii 104, 3, ; ix 73, 8.

** ix. 1, 36.

†† Rig-veda, i. 22.

clearly shows the indestructibility of the spirit. There are
also some passages which refer to the souls of deceased ancestors as still existing in another world.[*] It is scarcely
to be expected that in such primitive times they would
have very clear ideas on this subject ; but it is after all
worthy to be noticed that long before Greece and Rome
became cultivated communities, when Europe was the
home of uncivilized barbarians, the Ṛishis had some conception of this doctrine. Modern psychologists cannot
teach us more than what was taught by our ancestors
some thousand years ago. In the Brāhmaṇas immortality
is promised to those who rightly understand and regularly
practise the rites of sacrifice. Those who are deficient in
this respect and who depart to the next world before the
expiration of the natural term of life, are weighed there in
a balance.[†] The doctrine of the Brāhmaṇas is that after
death all are born again in the next world, where they are
recompensed according to their deeds ; the good being re-
warded, and the wicked punished.[‡] But elsewhere heaven
is said to belong only to the Brahmans.[§]

There are very few passages in the Brāhmaṇas which
proclaim the idea of absorption in the deity such as we find
in the Upaniṣhads. But from a passage in the Satapatha-
Brāhmaṇa we learn how in the next world the animals
and plants devour men who make a repast of them
in this state of existence ; unless they are resuscitated to life

[*] Ṛig-veda, i. 35, 16. ; iii. 55, 2 ; vi. 52, 4.

[†] Satapatha-Brāhmaṇa, xi. 2, 7, 33   Compare Proverbs, xvi. 2.

[‡] Ibid., vi. 2, 2, 27 ; x. 6, 3, 1 ; xi. 7, 3, 33.

[§] Aitareya-veda, i. 5, 1.

by the performance of usual ceremonies and sacrifices.[*]
The word *prâyaschitta* by which expiation or atonement
is implied, does not occur in the songs of the *Rig-veda*.
But it occurs often in the Brâhmanas and the Sûtras in
the sense of a means for removing a grievance, or avert-
ing an evil ; and not in the sense of an atonement for a
sin committed.

In the *Rig-veda* Yama is nowhere described in the
same manner as in the later mythology.[†] He is not represented there as a terrible being, but as the ruler of the
dead, possessing a beneficient character. He is said to
grant to the departed souls a resting place where they
may enjoy eternal happiness.[‡] Still he is to a certain extent an object of terror and horror. And in a passage of
the Atharvan death is said to be his messenger, who conveys the spirits of men to the abode of their forefathers.[§]
He is also said to have two formidable dogs with four eyes
and wide nostrils, which guard the road to his abode ;[||]
and he is asked to protect the departed from them.[¶]
The body which the soul is to take again in the
next world, cannot be the one which has undergone
cremation, or has been buried in the earth ; it may
not even be one similar to it, because he is to live
henceforth in the company of divine spirits, and so

[*] xi. 8, 1, 1 ff.
[†] Wilson's Vishnu-Purana, p. 216 of Dr. Hall's ed. vol. II.
[‡] Whitney's Oriental and Linguistic Studies, p 45.
[§] xviii. 2, 27.
[||] Rig-veda, x. 14, 10-12.
[¶] Rig-veda, x. 14, 11.

must have such a body as to have a right of place
among them.* It is said that the deceased will take his
new body, a shining and all glorious spiritual body.†
Nowhere in the *Rig-veda* is any trace discoverable of
metempsychosis :‡ which was, no doubt, gradually developed in India itself, but never was it introduced from
any foreign country.§ But, on the contrary, it is promised, as the highest reward, that the pious shall again
be born in the next world with his earthly body.‖ In
certain passages a hope is also held out that the family
relations will be maintained in the next world.¶

How the primitive religion and worship of the Indo-
Aryans gradually changed and became more and more
elaborate and complicated, may be best known from the
Vedas themselves. In a history of the ancient Sanskrit
literature the Chhandas period is the most interesting and
most important in a philosophical point of view. In the
Chhandas period, the state of society being simple, religious worship was necessarily so. Now the *Rishis* were

* Roth's article on the Morality of the Vedas in the Journal of the
American Oriental Society, III. p. 342. This paper is, in many respects,
very interesting. But there is a ludicrous inconsistency staring us in the
face. Poor Yama is charged with the attempt to seduce his sister. The
fact as the *Rig-veda* gives it was the reverse. The sister longed for co-
habitation with her brother, and arguing "for his consent to her wishes.
Strange, that Dr. Roth did not correct it.
† *Rig-veda*, x. 14, 8.
‡ Wilson's *Rig-veda*, id. p. xxii. Müller's Chips, i. p. 45.
§ Bunsen's Orient and Occident, III. p. 162. f.
‖ *Aitareya-Brahmana*, iv. 6, 1. 1 : xi. 2, 8. 6 ; xii. 8, 2, 31.
¶ *Atharva-veda*, xii. 8, 27 : vi. 120, 3.

the priests of their own families to which they imparted
religious instructions; and for which they conducted the
daily worship. But in the process of time such a religious worship underwent a gradual but marked change.
And as soon as we step into the Mantra and the Bráhmana
periods, we observe the gross superstitious character which
that primitive religion and worship gradually assumed.
In those periods a priesthood was systematically created;
and nothing could be done without a priest.

" A'svaláyana says that there were four chief priests;
each having three subordinate priests under him." And
these sixteen officiating priests are commonly called by
the general term of Ritvíj.† There were also a compli-
ment of assistants of these sixteen priests, who of course
did not rank as Ritvíj. The Kaushítakins alone admit
the so-called Sadasyas into the Ritvíj, whose sole business
was to superintend all the sacrifices. The priests had
peculiar duties to perform, which are prescribed in the
Bráhmanas. The Adhvaryus had to recite the verses of
the Yajur-veda, to measure the ground, to build the vedi,
or altar, to make the sacrificial vessels, to fetch wood and
water, to light the fire, to bring the animal and immolate
it. And certainly they constituted the lowest class of
priests. The Udgátris had to chant the songs of the Sáma-
veda, and to act as the chorus. The peculiar duty of the
Hotris was to recite in a distinct and loud voice certain

* Srauta-sútra, i. 1. See also Kátyáyana's Srauta-sútra, vii. 1. 6.
† Both's Sanskrit and Grimm Dictionary sub voce ritvij where
the appellations of the sixteen kinds of priests are given. See also the
passage in the Satapatha-Bráhmana, iii. 3 et seq., there referred to.

verses of the Rig-veda in praise of the deities during the time of sacrifices. The Hotris were no doubt, by far the most highly educated class of priests. The Brahmâ had to watch over these three classes of priests, and to remedy any defect which might affect the efficacy of the sacrifice. And the Rig-veda itself in one of its latest portions, recognises the superiority of the Brahmâ priest. He was supposed to know the whole ceremonial, and all the three Vedas used by the Hotris, Adhvaryus, and Udgâtris.* The office of a Brahmâ priest was not however a birth right; but every priest could obtain it by assiduous and unremitting study, great ability, and superior ingenuity. The most ancient name of a professional priest was Purohita; and he was more than a chaplain. He was the counsellor of a chief, and the minister of a king, and his companion, too, in peace and war. However, the original institution of a Purohita must not be accepted as a sign of a far advanced hierarchical system. But his office was undoubtedly regarded as a divine institution. Vasishtha and Viśvâmitra were the Purohitas of king Sudâs.† The chief occupation of the

* Müller's History of Ancient Sanskrit Literature, p. 485 f.

† Viśvâmitra, says Sigmer de Gubernatis (in the Rivista Orientale, I. pp. 169 f., 475 f.), is to be understood as one of the appellations of the sun; and as both the person who holds the moon, and Indra are the sons of Kasika, they must be brothers. Vasishtha is the greatest of the Vasus, and means Agni the early fire, and points out, like Viśvâmitra, to the sun. Sudâs signifies the brow of the sun, or the sun himself. Ancient Indian tradition speaks of both Viśvâmitra and Vasishtha as real historical personages. His theory, therefore, is quite untenable.

Purohita was simply to perform the ordinary sacrifices; but his office even partook of a political character. The ancient appellations of the theologians of the Rik as Bahvvichas, those of the Sāman as Chhandogas, and of the Yajus as Adhvaryus are to be found in the Samhitā of the Black Yajus and in the Satapatha-Brāhmana. The Black Yajus applies the term Adhvaryus to its own adherents, whilst their opponents are called Charakā-dhvaryus. This natural hustility is also clearly shown in a passage of the Samhitā of the White Yajus.* But this spirit of hostility was not exclusively confined to the different schools of the Yajur-veda; the followers of the Atharva-veda seem to have betrayed similar sectarian jealousies towards the adherents of the other Vedas.†

The term Brahman originally denoted devout worshippers and contemplative sages or poets, who composed hymns in praise of the gods. But after the ceremonial of worship became highly developed and complicated, and the sacred functions became quite distinct from other occupations, the epithet gradually came to be employed for a minister of religion, and at last it came to signify one particular class of priests with certain special duties. Then the hierarchy of the Brahmans was completely organised. Though now priesthood formed an exclusive caste, which for the most part became an hereditary order; yet those among other classes that aspired to sacerdotal

* Weber's History of Indian Literature, p. 87; Müller's History of Ancient Sanskrit Literature, p. 350.
† Weber's Indische Studien, i. p. 296.

functions and privileges, were also admitted to the same order. Of course as a class some of them were intelligent, some unintelligent, some thoughtful, and some as mere mechanical instruments at the celebration of ceremonial worship.[*] However, great benefits are said to have resulted from the employment of priests[†] as their presence was deemed an essential condition of the efficacy of the ritual acts ; and even the highest efficacy is said to result from their intercession.[‡] Liberality to them is also mentioned with approbation.[§] A superhuman power was ascribed to the priests ;[||] and curses were fulminated against their oppressors.[¶] But the comparison of frogs to them implies a total disregard for them and for their functions.[**] The sacred and divinely consecrated majesty of the priests was not unfrequently assailed by the ungodly ; and consequently they had to encounter much difficulty to enforce a due regard which they themselves attached to the performance of religious rites. And we then find a long list of condemnatory epithets applied to those persons who were the deniers of the gods, and who were averse to the rites. The Kalpa works enjoin that the Hotri is to perform his duties with the Rik, the

[*] Rigveda, vii. 50, 9.

[†] Atharvaveda, III. 19.

[‡] Rigveda, vii. 63, 6.

[§] Rigveda, i. 125 ; i. 126 ; v. 27 ; v. 30, 12 ff. ; v. 61, 10 ; vi. 27, 8 ; vi. 47, 22 ff.

[||] Atharvaveda, xix. 9, 12 ; xix. 42, 8.

[¶] Atharvaveda, xii. 5.

[**] Rigveda, vii. 103.

Udgâtri with the Sâman, the Adhvaryu with the Yajus, and the Brahmâ with all the three Vedas.

Religion is nothing without a worship and without a cultus ; and, in fact, the origin and growth of sacrifice is an important page in the history of the human mind. The chapter on sacrifices may be dull, monotonous and uninteresting ; but by a critical examination of them we are enabled to determine step by step the different stages of civilization, through which the eastern branch of the whole Aryan family passed. Some sacrifices, no doubt, belong to the pastoral stage of civilization, some to the agricultural stage of civilization, and some attest to the chivalrous character of the times. The Smârta-sacrifices were such as properly belonged to the pastoral and agricultural stages of civilization. But the Srauta-sacrifices could be performed only by a prosperous community at once chivalrous and enterprising. The Soma-sacrifices belonged to the period of chivalry ; and the Rig-veda also abounds in passages which at once exhibit the chivalrous character of the times. The system of Vaidik sacrifices throws an immense light on many a dark point in the history of the Indo-Aryans ; and there is no doubt that the sacrifices, upon the whole, exercised a most potent influence upon their social and religious polity. Sacrifices were not all for the first time instituted in India ; but a good many were brought from their cradle in central Asia where they must have passed through those stages before emigration took place. In India certainly those rites and ceremonies again underwent radical and most extensive changes. In the earlier part of the Vaidik times the first duty which the Indo-Aryans owed to their gods, was the performance of their worship with its ceremonies; and that form of worship, no doubt, was simple, patriarchal and domestic. It was performed three times daily simply with hymns and prayers very often accompanied with fruits and the products of the flocks which were offered on the family altars. This established order of worship with its ceremonies is called rita. The ceremonial worship was not left to the charge of the priests; it was but a spontaneous act of devotion, and was neither tedious nor complicated in its minor details. But when in the course of time the priests formed themselves into a privileged class worship and ceremonies underwent immense modifications. And thus most of the rites gradually required the sacrifice of a large number of various kinds of beasts and birds. The rites, offerings, oblations and sacrifices were all performed with the distinct purpose either to avert an evil or to secure a coveted object by divine intercession, or to propitiate the gods themselves. They were offered to gain the good will of some offended deity, or through the dread of others.

At the celebration of the Darsapurnamas sacrifice the Adhvaryus had to place the cows and calves together, and to touch the calves with the branch of a tree. This sacrifice was celebrated at new and full moon. Besides this, we have innumerable names of sacrifices; of which the Rājasūya, Agnihotra, Asvamedha, Somayāga and Purushamedha are by far the most remarkable. The Asvamedha or horse-sacrifice was probably adopted by the Indians from the Scythians, before they crossed the Indus.[*] At this sacrifice 609 animals of various descriptions, domestic and wild, were tied to 21 posts, but after the customary prayers had been offered up, they were three times led round the sacrificial fire. Elephants, camels,[†] buffaloes, birds, porpoises, crocodiles, snakes, and even mosquitoes and worms were included among the animals. At last the horse was immolated by an axe, and its flesh was cut up into fragments, dressed, partly roasted, and partly boiled, and made into balls and eaten. This ceremony was subsequently performed symbolically.[‡] The sacrifice of the horse, and that of the cow, no doubt, were common in the earliest periods of the Vaidik ritual. The Brāhmaṇs of the Black Yajus and both the Kalpa and the Grihya-sūtras distinctly mention the different occasions when cattle should be slaughtered and eaten. It is no less a fact that the meat of cattle was required for the due celebration of some of other ceremonies; and more particularly the Rājasūya, the Vājapeya, the Aśvamedha, the Panchaśradīya sava, and the Sūla gava could not have been performed without it. The proper place for the performance of the Sūla gava rite was outside a village or a town, unfrequented by men, and the time was after midnight. The Gomedha was not certainly typical as many are disposed to believe. The Navamanayana was held for four days. It formed a part of the Mahā-

[*] Herodotus, iv. 71.
[†] Compare Sanskrit krameda and Greek kamelos.
[‡] Wilson's Introduction to the Rig-veda.

plava, Dvādaśāha, and a few other ceremonies; but it
did not constitute a distinct rite by itself. The Sarvamedha or All-sacrifice and the Brahmayajña are passed over
in the Śatapatha-Brāhmaṇa. They find place in the
Āraṇyaka of the Taittirīyas, but not in their Brāhmaṇa.
The Pitrimedha or Sacrifice to the Manes has place in the
Āraṇyaka as well as in the Brāhmaṇa of the Taittirīyas.
The Puruṣhamedha or Man-sacrifice required the actual
sacrifice of man; and it had for its distinct object the
acquisition of independent sovereignty over all created
beings. But in reality it was entirely of an expiatory nature.
It required full forty days for its celebration; and a hundred
and eighty-five men of various tribes, characters, and
professions were essentially required to be bound to eleven
posts and consecrated to various deities. The holocausts
of human victims formed part of the ancient cultus of
India; and there is a strong presumptive evidence that
Sanaḥśepa was intended for an actual immolation. It is
beyond doubt that the Indo-Aryans were familiar with
the idea of human sacrifice.* It also found favor with
the Druids, the Scythians, and the Phoenicians; and some
traces of it are found even in the Bible. The earliest indication of the rite occurs in the Rig-veda, in the Vājas-
neyi-Saṃhitā of the White Yajur-veda and the Śatapatha-
Brāhmaṇa. The Aitareya and the Taittirīya-Brāhmaṇas
also refer to it.

* Wilson's Essay on Human Sacrifice in the Veda; Roth, in Weber's
Indische Studien, I. pp. 457-464; and II. pp. 111-123; Weber's History
of Indian Literature, p. 84.

a

The principal object for which the Sáma-veda was composed, was the performance of those sacrifices in which the juice of the Soma plant was principally required. And of such sacrifices the most remarkable is the Jyotish-toma, which consists of seven stages; but the celebration of the first stage or the Agnishtoma alone was deemed obligatory, while the other six stages, such as the Atyag-nishtoma, Ukthya, Shodasin, Atirātra, Aptoryāma, and Vājapeya, though adding to the virtue of the sacrificer, were considered as voluntary. The Soma was from the earliest times connected with the religious history of the Indo-Aryans;* and was thus elevated to the proud position of a god. The Rig-veda is replete with its praises; and the other three Vedas also contain mantras to be recited at all the stages of its manufacture. The high antiquity of this cultus is attested by the references to it to be found in the Zend-Avesta.† The plants were gathered by the roots on the hills on a moonlight night, and after being stripped of their leaves they were brought in carts drawn by two rams or he-goats to the house of the sacrificer. The stalks then were deposited in the hall of oblation, and bruised and crushed between stones, and placed with the juice in a sieve of goats' hair, and were further pressed

---

* Windischmann's Dissertation on the Soma worship of the Aryans; Whitney's Main Results of the Later Vedic Researches in Germany; Lassen's Indian Antiquities, i. p. 518; and Roth's articles in the Journal of the German Oriental Society, for 1848 (pp. 216ff.) and 1850 (pp. 117 ff.)

† Plutarch de Isid. et Osir. 46, in which the Soma, or as it is in Zend, haoma, appears to be referred to under the appellation of omomi.

and squeezed by the priests' ten fingers one or two of which being ornamented by rings of flattened gold. Finally, the juice mixed with barley, wheat, and clarified butter was allowed to ferment; and was then drawn off in a scoop called *srooh*, and offered up thrice daily to the gods, and a ladleful was taken by the priests. From the Vaidik descriptions of the effects of the Soma nectar on the gods, to whom it was the most acceptable and delightful oblation, we are to believe that it was a fermented intoxicating beverage; and this again we can assume from our knowledge of the effects produced by its use in men. The expressed juice of the Soma creeper itself had not either its narcotic property or its keeping quality; but it being diluted with water, mixed with clarified butter, barley meal, and the meal of wild paddy or *nivara*, and at last being left to ferment in a jar for nine days, it acquired its exhilarating and inebriating effects.* While it was invested with a sacramental and religious character, it was by no means manufactured for sale. But it was in all cases preserved in a bag of *cowskin*.†

* Stevenson's Sáma-veda, p. 32-d; Roer's Aitareya-Bráhmana, i. p. 6; Manning's Ancient India, i. p. 82.

† Rig-veda, v. 8, 10.

————

CHAPTER III.

*General Character of the Vedas—the Vaidik Dialect—
and the Chronology of the Vaidik Age.*

Sir William Jones said that the student of Indo-
Aryan literature and religion found himself in the presence of infinity. As Homer was the sole repository of
intellectual culture in Greece, so the Vedas are here in
India. The original texts of the four Vedas, and the immense body of literary records which had grouped themselves about them by gradual accretion, form a bulk so
incredibly vast and of such enormous importance that
not the whole body of sacred literature of any one ancient nation can be compared with that of the Indo-Aryans.
Whatever was handed down, as a sacred trust, from father
to son, soon received a kind of hallowed character; and
also derived its importance from the circumstance to
which its origin was due. Our Aryan fathers handed to
us the scriptural Vedas, which have been canonised as
time wore on; and which, notwithstanding many pueri-
lities and repulsive legends, arrest our thoughts and
inspire us with keen interest. They looked upon their
venerated scriptures as the foundation of their power and

prestige. Our heart grows warm when we find the
Vedas to be strewn with original and at the same time
sober and profound ideas, pure and sublime conceptions,
and lofty sentiments which were by no means unworthy of
our most distant ancestors. In them we read at any rate
the reflex of the laws and thoughts of a divine being; and
they seem to contain the thread which links the present
with the past. To the Vedas must be attached an undying
interest and an ever increasing value not only for their
greatest antiquity, but also for the immense flood of light
which they throw on the primitive state of the Indo-Aryan
society, Indo-Aryan speech, and general mythology. We
do not yet find in them any traces of a growing religion
or a growing language; nevertheless we gain from them a
real insight into the feelings, the aspirations, the thoughts,
the fears, the hopes, the doubts, and the faith of our
ancestors. And in process of time the Vaidik religion,
whatever it was, has become, through the corruptions and
prejudices, of a most revolting type, of successive ages,
a heterogeneous medley of theology, philosophy and
science.

Beyond doubt, India with her ancient and illustrious
name hoary with hallowed traditions, claims a very high
antiquity as well as a distinguished rank among the civilised countries of the ancient world. But unfortunately,
there is nothing historical in Sanskrit literature which
records the heroic exploits of the Indo-Aryans;[*] and the
word *history* itself is unknown in their language. Indeed, the Indo-Aryans never possessed any true 'historical

* Burnouf's History of Indian Buddhism, p. iii.

sense.' However, to get an insight into the state of the civilization of the Vaidik age, it is necessary that we should refer to the pages of the Vedas themselves. The Vedas are the ancient Shatra of the Indo-Aryans, or, as now they are called, the Hindus.† The Vedas are far

* The word Veda is derived from the Sanskrit root *vid*, to know, and is the same with the Greek *id*, Latin *vid*, Gothic *vait*; and may be translated into *learning* or *knowledge*.

† It is interesting to inquire into the origin of the term *Hindu*. It occurs with the whole treasure of Sanskrit words in the Sabda-kalpa-Druma, and therefore it may seem to many that it is of Sanskrit origin. But the authority which has been cited in it from the Merutantra, xxiii, to prove that it is such, shows, on the contrary, that it is a modern word. In fact, the Tantras are wanting in the title of antiquity. The oldest among them, says Dr. Rájendralála Mitra, was not composed before the 3rd century of Christ, and the majority of them probably between the 6th and the 13th century. There is, however, a word equivalent to the national name in the Zend. And it also re-appears as Hindu for Hindu in a portion of the Hebrew scriptures called Esther. The term Hindu is not found to appear in any of the ancient Sanskrit authors. Indeed, this word was never employed in the Sanskrit language. But nevertheless it is not of very modern origin. Herodotus (iv. 44 : v. 3) has noticed the Hindus under the general appellation of *Indoi*. The word Hindu was derived from Sindhu; and the ancient Persians must have at first used that term, as it is established and it cannot be gainsaid, that according to Zend grammar the term Hindu owes its origin to Sindhu or Hindu as pronounced by them. In the Vendidid (i. 73) we have the expression Hapta-Hindu which is nothing more than a transformation of the Sanskrit Sapta-Sindhavas, the land of the seven rivers, which was a designation of the Vaidik India. It was also very well known to the Romans in the days of Augustus (Virgil's Æneid, ix. 30). In the Cuneiform Inscriptions Hidus is used for Sapta-Sindhavas, and it should be so understood. — See Spiegel's Avesta, i. p. 66, note 2.

unlike the Qur'ān as "an endless incoherent rhapsody of fable and precept, and declaration, which seldom excites a sentiment or an idea, which sometimes crawls in the dust and is sometimes lost in the clouds."[*] That our ancestors looked on the Vedas with the greatest possible reverence is no marvel. The Vedas were, no doubt, their first national efforts in the department of literature. In them we catch astronomical observations in their primary stage, philosophical thoughts in their first dawn, mythology in the course of formation, poetry gradually rising to unmistakeable excellence ; and even the first attempts in the department of grammar and glossary. And they reflect the growth and development of the national life of the Aryan world. It is our belief that no service more important could be rendered to the history of our race, than to diffuse the knowledge and encourage the investigation of the Vaidik writings.

The Vedas which stand at the head of the whole body of Indian literature, are altogether a peculiar class of writings. They are each, upon the whole, composed of the same identical matter ; they also harmonise with one another in external form and language, and even in the nature of their contents. But when we take into consideration such other matters as are their peculiar characteristics, internal arrangement, the date, and object of collection, and their use at the worship of the various gods, or at some of the ceremonials having close relation with various grand events in the domestic or public life of the

* Gibbon's Roman Empire. i. p. 269.

Indo-Aryans, they appear respectively to be of an altogether dissimilar character.

The word Veda is significantly employed to designate those ancient Samskrit works, in which is laid the foundation of Brahmanic belief; and these works were originally three, i. e., the Rig-veda, the Sama-veda, and the Yajur-veda. The frequent mention of the Indian scriptures is made in ancient Samskrit literature under the name of *trai-vidyá*, or the triple science.[*] The Veda is and remains three-fold; and the triple Veda is comprehended under the name of *mantra*. But at a more subsequent period a fourth Veda was added to them; though it was never held as sacred as its predecessors were. However, they are now commonly four in number, viz., the Rig-veda—Veda of hymns, the Sama-veda—Veda of chants, the Yajur-veda—Veda of sacrificial formulas, and the Atharva-veda—Veda of incantations. Manu, in his Institutes, often speaks of the three first Vedas calling them *trayam brahma sanátanam*;[†] and he mentions only once (xi. 35) "the revelations of the Atharvángirasas" alluding to, but not designating by name, the Atharva-veda. Amara Sinha, in his Kosha, also notices only three Vedas;[‡] but refuses the Atharvan a place among them. The Atharva-veda is not mentioned in the Chhándogya-upanishad (iv. 17, 1); and the Kaushítaki-Bráhmana also omits to mention it.[§] But in the Atharva-

---

[*] Satapatha-Bráhmana, iv. 6, 7, 1; Aitareya-Bráhmana, v. 32.

[†] Manu I. 23.

[‡] त्रयी वेद वेद वयूनी इति तै द्रायव वर्षी ।

[§] Müller's History of Ancient Samskrit Literature, p. 457.

veda itself it is reckoned among the Vedas under the
designation of the Atharvas and Angirasos (x. 7, 20);
and it is similarly alluded to in the Satapatha-Brāhmaṇa
(xiii. 4, 3, 7). And in the ninth verse of the Purusha-
sūkta it is even mentioned and designated under the title
of Chhandas. "The true reason why the three first
Vedas are often mentioned without any notice of the
fourth, must be sought, not in their different origin and
antiquity, but in the difference of their use and purport."[*]

The Rig-veda is extant only in the recension of the Śāk-
alas; and we have only references to the other recension of
the Vāshkalas. But the difference between the two was
not very considerable; the Vāshkalas had only eight hymns
more. Although the greater portion of the hymns of the
Rik-Samhitā was composed on the banks of the Indus;
their final redaction certainly took place in India proper
during the period when the Brahmanical element had
become predominant; and the Kosala-Videhas and the
Kuru-Panchālas had the chief merit of having effected it.[†]
The Rik is to the student of history the Veda par excellence.
The Rig-veda is no less a repository of the hymns which
were composed after our early ancestors had reached the
land of their adoption, and with which they addressed the
gods in whom they believed, and extolled other matters
with a spontaneous freshness and simplicity, than it is a
store-house of also those hymns which they had brought
with them as the most precious heirloom from their

* Colebrooke's Essays. i. p 13.
† Weber's History of Indian Literature, pp. 30 ff.

ancient home to the West.° The hymns which they brought with them were preserved in families as single and unconnected compositions for several centuries solely by tradition, and thus they must have undergone an amount of wear and tear; and Prof. Aufrecht very justly remarks that possibly only a small portion of such hymns may have been preserved to us in the Rik.† The Rig-veda consists, with a few exceptions, of detached prayers dedicated to divinities now no longer worshipped, some of whom are even entirely unknown. And in point of time and even literary development it is the oldest of books and the earliest depository of Aryan faith. The Yajus, the Sâman, and the Atharvan presuppose the Rik; and the anteriority of the Rik to the Brâhmanas is proved not only by the frequent allusions which are made to the former by the latter, but also by the words and phrases employed in the hymns themselves. The language and style of the Rik is artificial, and its poetry is utterly deficient in natural sublimity; there is, however, one redeeming feature in it namely that most of the hymns contain moral ideas and spiritual hopes and aspirations. Though there is little that is attractive and beautiful in the Rik, and though some of its hymns are utterly insipid and have no life or meaning at all; yet the volume itself gives life to antiquity, and gives us a real and living idea of our early ancestors. As a complete panorama of

° Langlois, Preface to his French translation of the Rig-veda, I pp. x. xi. See also Journal of the American Oriental Society, iv. p. 249.

† Weber's Indische Studien, iv. p. 8.

ancient religion it reveals to us the very beginnings of human life and thought. Fortunately, there is no system in the Rik.

The Rik-Samhitā is a lyrical collection; and these lyrics are of the simplest form. We hardly find in it high flights of poetical fancy; and there is least trace of abstraction. There is no doubt that it was composed in the infancy of the human race. As a real stratum of ancient thought and religion, the Rik contains many things which are now quite unintelligible to us. The Rik however contains some really historical elements; and Prof. Roth very justly calls it the historical Veda. The Rik is evidently composed of heterogeneous materials. Its first seven books bear a similar character, arranged upon a like plan. These books embrace the oldest, the most genuine and the most sacred hymns; and retain, as far as the tradition goes, an integral and not incongruous whole; and palpably remain as it was originally fixed and arranged. The eighth and ninth books present quite a different system of internal arrangement. The tenth book corresponds with the arrangement of two of its predecessors, and copiously supplies us with the most distinct evidences of a later origin. In various instances, the tradition is very unreliable with reference to the authorship of the hymns, and even in certain cases it is found to attribute some of them to mythical personages.

The hymns now united into a Samhitā, had existed in detached forms, and were preserved as sacred heirlooms in different families, before they were aggregated together and arranged in the order in which we now find them. The

hymns are arranged in the order of the deities addressed,
and in accordance with the families of various rishis
which are credited with their authorship. And this
classification is no doubt based upon a scientific principle.
It is very probable, that the redaction of the text may
have taken place at a later date than those of the Sáman
and of the Yajus. The first eight books comprise hymns
which are addressed to Agni, Indra, the Viswa-devás
and other divinities. The ninth is solely dedicated to
Soma, which has the closest connexion with the
Sáman ; whereas the tenth mainly supplied the materials
for the Atharva-veda. The same hymn which is dedicated
to the same deity, is, however, sometimes addressed to
different divinities. Many hymns also partake of the
nature of petitions or panegyrics addressed to eminent
chiefs or heroes either living or dead. But the general form
of the hymns is dialogistic. The hymns are to be understood as combining the attributes of both prayer and
praise ; and in them the goodness, the generosity,
the power, the vastness, and even the personal beauty
of the deities are described with no end of rhetorical
flourish. And also these deities are besought to confer
blessings which are for the most part of a worldly and
physical character : as food, wealth, a long life, a large
family, power, cattle, cows, horses, protection against enemies, complete victory over them, and sometimes their utter
destruction.* But the hymns themselves afford no directions for their employment, and make no mention of the

* Wilson's Rig-veda, i. p. xxii ff ; Roth's Literature and History of the
Veda, p. 4.

occasions on which they are to be applied, or of the ceremonies at which they are to be chanted.*

A large number of hymns of the Rik-Samhitā are
repeated in the other Vedas; while none of the verses
which properly belong to the latter are to be met
with in the former. The collection of the richas in
a systematic form should be attributed rather to
more scientific causes. And we may even suppose that
science in this case may have overdone her work; and
instead of subjecting the hymns to a considerable modification, may have also improved upon them, and so transmitted to us a *rifacimento*.

We find in the Rik-Samhitā a few hymns known by the
name of *Khilas*, which were added at the end of each chapter after the whole collection of the ten books had been
completed. The *Khilas*, as the Vaidik apocrypha, must be
looked upon as a link closely connecting the Vaidik hymns
with the latter parts of the Indo-Aryan literature. We are
only to accept them as successful imitations of the real and
genuine songs; but as such they acquired a certain degree
of sanctity and dignity. They also gradually crept into
the Samhitās of the other Vedas; they are even referred
to in the Brāhmaṇas, although they are not counted
in the Anukramaṇīs. There is also another class of hymns
called *dānastutis* or praises of certain kings for their gifts
to the priests.† These hymns wear, upon the whole, a
modern character; and they may be assigned to the
latter part of the Mantra period.

---

* Wilson's Rig-veda. i. p. viii.   † Colebrooke's Essays, i. p. 22.

H

The *Rik-Samhita* is certainly a wonderful work ; and proves that the Indo-Aryan mind had been scientifically developed long before the age of the poems of Homer or Hesiod. It must not be assumed that the hymns of this Veda are purely of a religious character. A hymn in the seventh book recounts in a singularly jocular manner the revival of the frogs at the commencement of the rains, and likens their croaking to the singing of the Brahmans in ceremonial worships.[*] It is certainly a curious fact that the same animal was selected by the earliest satirist of Greece as the representative of the Homeric heroes.[†] Again, in the tenth book we have the lamentation of a gamester over his ruinous devotion to play.[‡] Numerous other instances of a similar nature might be easily adduced. In all probability these portions, which are considered as non-religious, belong to a later period.

The hymns of the *Rik* themselves are apparently of different periods spreading over several centuries ; some among them being older and some more recent.[§] When we read of any *Rishi* speaking of his own hymn as new, we must conclude that he was of course acquainted with

[*] *Rig-veda*, vii. 103

[†] Müller's Ancient Sanskrit Literature, pp. 494 f

[‡] *Rig-veda* x. 34

[§] i. 12, 11 ; i. 47, 4 ; i. 60, 3 , i. 89, 3 , i. 96, 3 , i 130, 10 , i. 143, 1 ; ii. 17, 1 ; ii. 81, 1 ; iii. 1, 20 , vi. 17, 13 , vi. 22, 7 , vi. 44, 13 ; vii. 48, 11 , vii. 50, 6. Max Müller designates the most ancient portion of the hymns by the term *Chhandas*, and those that are comparatively modern, *Mantra* (see his History of Ancient Sanskrit Literature, pp. 70, 525 ff). But it is to be observed that he is altogether singular in the use of these two words in the above sense as they nowhere obtain in the ancient Sanskrit

many of the older hymns of the same kind. The relative antiquity of the different hymns can only be determined by their general contents, ideas, language, style and metre.[*] The old hymns, however, were displaced by the new ; but the former were held as sacred as the latter. The authors of the new hymns had to borrow many thoughts and words from the old ones ; and such repetitions often occur in their compositions.[†] And the proof of the antiquity of the Vaidik hymns lies in the fact that many words used in the Veda afterwards became obsolete. Then, in fact, the refinements of grammar had no existence. The hymns are drawn up in a great variety of metres, most of which are peculiar to them. The metres an employed show a long and successful cultivation of the rhythmical art

writers. Excepting the Brahmana portion the rest is generally called Mantra. In the Purusha-sukta (x. 90) even Chhandas is put for the Atharvan ; and the Atharvan itself is also referred to under the same designation in one of its own verses (xi 7, 24). Yaska in his portion repeatedly speaks of the Vedas in the general term of Chhandas though indicating sometimes the Mantra portion, and sometimes even the Brahmana portion (Goldstucker's Panini, p. 71). In the entire collection of ancient and modern Sanskrit literature, Chhandas is applied exclusively to the whole body of the Veda. But Chhandas is nowhere employed for the most ancient portions of the Veda nor Mantra for those that are comparatively modern. Muller (Chips, I. p. 84) further considers that Zend and Chhandas are both equivalent terms ; Zend being a corruption of the Sanskrit Chhandas. Although they seem to resemble in sound and letter, yet there is nothing of affinity in signification. Zend is used in the sense of commentary, explanation, or gloss ; while Chhandas in the ancient writers means sutra.

[*] Muir's Original Sanskrit Texts, III. p. 224.
[†] Langlois, Rig-veda, I. p. xiii.

We meet with the technical names of the metres in the latter portions of the Rik. And the entire body of hymns abound also in similes or metaphors distinguished by a vein of naive observations ; which certainly show a considerable amount of shrewdness and worldly wisdom possessed by the Indo-Aryans. It is, however, beyond doubt that the aggregate assemblage of hymns which comprises the Rik-Samhitá, could never have been composed by the men of one or even two generations ; and it is to be especially observed here in connexion with this point that there are hymns composed by the sons as well as by their fathers and earlier ancestors ;[*] and this fact is amply borne out by the passages of the hymns themselves which make an apparent distinction between the Rishis as ancient and modern. This acknowledgment attests to the existence of the historical element in the Veda. It is, of course, an acknowledgment on the part of the hymnists themselves that numerous persons had existed ; and a series of events occurred long before their own age.[†] The line which apparently separated the moderns from the ancients was undoubtedly traced by the immigration of the Indo-Aryans into India ; which was regarded by them as the greatest event in their annals, and which marked a new epoch in their chronology. It is most probable that several centuries must have elapsed between the composition of the oldest and that of the most recent richas ; and in this intervening period the Indo-Aryan community passed through

[*] i. 1, 2; i. 48, 14; i. 119, 3; i. 131, 6; ii. 80, 1; vi. 21, 1; vi. 42, 2; vii. 53, 1; vii. 76, 4; ix. 110, 7; x. 14, 15.

[†] Muir's Original Sanskrit Texts, iii. p. 219.

various stages of development, social, moral, religious
and intellectual.

The first book of the Rik-Samhitá contains one
hundred and ninety-one hymns which are with some
exceptions, ascribed to fifteen different authors such as
Gotama, Kaava, Kutsa, Sunahsepa, Kakshivan, Agastya,
&c. The second containing forty-three hymns is attributed
to Gritsamada ; the third, sixty-two, to Viswámitra ; the
fourth, fifty-eight to Vámadeva ; the fifth, eighty-seven,
to Atri ; the sixth, seventy-five, to Bharadvája ; the
seventh, one hundred and four, to Vasishtha ; the eighth,
which is entitled pragáthás, ninety-two, (besides 11 Vál-
khilya-sûktas) to Kaava ; the ninth, one hundred and
fourteen, to Angiras ; and the tenth, one hundred and
ninety-one, to Rishis of different families and also to
mythical personages. The names of the authors are
given here ; however by these names we are to understand even their families. The Sûktas or hymns again
are distinguished by different names, such as Mahá-
sûkta, Kakshira-sûkta, Madhyam-sûkta, Rishi-sûkta,
Devatá-sûkta, and Chhandas-sûkta ; and these terms
are applied simply to designate a certain scientific arrangement of the entire mass of the sûktas specially with
reference to the deity, author, metre, and quantity of
richas of each of them. The worship to which some of
the hymns of the Rik are devoted, must have been purely
of a sacrificial character ; and such worship consisted
more of detached sacrificial ceremonials than of a series of
sacrifices of a complicated character. Yet, there are to be
found hymns, which apparently indicate the existence, at

the time of their composition, of highly complicated and artificial rituals. But it does not, therefore, follow that the Rik as such, was drawn up for the purpose of being chanted at these rituals. The Yajur-veda and the Sāma-veda are indispensable for liturgic purposes; but, such is not the case with the Rik. The Rik must have preceded the completion of these ritual acts. Though many of the verses of the Rik are used at religious rites, yet there remain a good many which have no such purposes; and these verses are purely of a poetical or mystical character. Again, the Yajur-veda and the Sāma-veda are arranged in conformity with the sacrificial acts to which they apply; but the arrangement followed in the Rik is altogether different from them, and not with reference to such acts. The Rik, therefore, cannot have borne originally a ritual stamp.

The Sāma-veda is an anthology, and purely a derivative production. This Veda was at one time the most comprehensive of the four Vedas. It is more copious than the Yajus and the Atharvan, though not equal to the Rik. It is, however, nothing more than a reset of the Rik, being composed, with some exceptions, of the very same hymns, which are in their rich-form, although with the sāman-accents. The Sāman is also remarkably deficient in literary and historical interest. Burnell[*] and Aufrecht[†] urge against the superior antiquity of the readings of the Sāman, as compared with those of the Rik-Samhitā. The Sāma-Samhitā has come down to us in two recensions; one of which belongs to the school of the

* Aitareya-Brāhmaṇa, p. xvi ff.
† Hymns to the Rig-veda, pp. xvi, xvii.

Rânâyanîyas, and the other to that of the Kanthumas. These recensions, upon the whole, differ very little from each other. The Sâman consists of two parts :—the A'rchika or Pûrvârchika, also called Chhandograntha ; and Stau-bhika or Uttarârchika, also called Uttarâgrantha. The A'rchika which is arranged into fifty-nine decades and divided into chapters and half-chapters, is composed of five hundred and eighty-five verses, of which five hundred and thirty-nine are taken from the Rik ; and as adapted to the general and frequent use of the priests, exists in two forms, called Gânas, the Grâmageya-gâna (erroneously called Veya-gâna) which is divided into seventeen prapâthakas ; and the A'ranya-gâna into six prapâthakas. The A'ranya comprises songs adapted for recitation in forests ; and the Veya-gâna embraces such songs as are to be chanted in towns. The Staubhika which is distributed over nine chapters and subdivided into half-chapters, contains twelve hundred and twenty-five verses, of which eleven hundred and ninety-four are ap-propriated from the Rik. This portion exists in the same manner in two forms, called the U'ha-gâna which is divided into twenty-three prapâthakas ; and the U'hya-gâna into six prapâthakas. The Sâman, however, con-tains no indication which may determine approxi-mately the period of its origin. This Veda among other Vedas has a peculiar feature of its own in as much as it is provided with a system of accents which consist of no less than ten different signs. The chief object of this collec-tion must have been, as it appears from its special charac-teristics, that its riches should be chanted during the cere-

monies of Soma offering and on different other ceremonial
occasions. The verses contained in the Sâman are arranged according to their subjects; and the principal metres
employed in the whole collection are the Gâyatri, Vrihati,
Trishtubh, Anushtubh, Jagati, Barhari, Kakva, and Paakti.
The songs are consecrated to Agni, Indra, Prajâpati, Soma,
Varuna, Tvasti, Angiri, Pushâ, Sarasvati and Indrâgni.
And the style of the Veda is, upon the whole, very
antiquated.

Prof. Benfey has shown in the preface (p. xix.) to his
valuable edition of the Sâma-Samhita that there exist in
it some verses, the absence of which in the Rik is conspicuous. The total absence of seventy-one verses as found
in the recensions of the Sâman, from the recension in
which we now possess the Rik-Samhita, must only be
accounted for by the circumstance, that these verses belonged in fact to one or the other of the recensions of the Rik,
which have now altogether perished.* The relation of
the Sâman with the Rik is to a certain degree analogous
to that between the White and the Black Yajus.† The
Sâman and the Yajus are the attendants of the Rik.‡ The
Sâman cannot be considered as an enlargement of the original Veda; but the case of the Yajus is quite different. Both contain different readings varying in greater or less degree from those of the Rig-Veda Samhita. The richas occuring in the Sâma-Veda Samhita

* Müller's History of Ancient Sanskrit Literature, p. 475.
† Weber's Indische Studien, I. p. 69 ff.
‡ Kaushitaki-Brâhmana, vi 11 . या,हिरण्यगर्भिणी देवी ।

and the Yajuh-Samhitá are, with some exceptions, borrowed
in an altered form from the Rik-Samhitá; and these detached richas again appear to exhibit very little harmony
with the text of the latter. But the richas found in the
Sáman are to be taken as older and more original on account of the greater antiquity of their grammatical forms
than those of the two Samhitás of the Yajus where they
have undergone a secondary modification.* Some of the
Sútras of the Sáman are little more than lists, such as we
find in the Anukramanis, appended to the Vedas. Their
style, upon the whole, very nearly approaches the style of
the Sútra works.

The Yajur-veda is in a double form: the Black Yajus
or the Taittiriya-Samhitá and the White Yajus or the
Vájasaneyi-Samhitá. These, in the main, have the same
matter; but they seem to differ from each other only as
regards their details and arrangement. In the Black
Yajus the formulas for the entire sacrificial ceremonial
are generally accompanied by dogmatical explanations,
and ritual supplements; while in the White Yajus the
case is quite different. There they form subjects that are
entirely distinct from one another. The Black Yajus is
the older of the two.† The White embraces texts which
are not found in the Black; and when viewed in reference to the motley character of the latter the former
looks 'white,' or orderly. The White is manifestly intended as an improvement on the Black. But these two

* Weber's History of Indian Literature, p. 9.
† Colebrooke's Literary Remains, i. p. 57.

different divisions must have displayed a good deal of
antagonism towards each other." The Black and the
White Yajus originated, no doubt, with a schism of
which Yajnavalkya was most probably the author.† They
originated in the eastern parts of Hindustan, in the country of the Kurupanchalas, and they belong to a period
when the Brahmanical organization and the system of
caste were completely consolidated.‡ Three different
recensions of the Black Yajus are known to us; one that
of A'pastamba, a sub-division of the Khandikiyas; the
other, the Kathaka, which belongs to the school of the
Charakas; and another the A'treya, a sub-division of the
Aukhiyas. The A'pastambiyas belong to southern India,
and their founder was a native of A'ndhra country or the
districts between the Godavari and the Krishna.§ The existence of the A'ndhra kingdom was also known to Pliny.‖
The Samhita of the Black Yajus is in fact a medley of un-
digested fragments of all sorts. It comprises seven kándas
or books; these again include forty-four prapáthakas or
chapters, embracing altogether six hundred and fifty-one
anuvákas or sections, which are arranged in two thousand,
one hundred and ninety-eight kandikas or portions. The
recensions of the White Yajus bear the names of the

* Weber's Indische Studien, i. p. 294.
† Wilson's Works, v. p. 332.
‡ Weber's History of Indian Literature, p. 107.
§ Cunningham's Geography. p. 527 supp., Burnell's South Indian
Palæography, p. 14, note 2.
‖ Pliny, Hist. Nat. vi. 22.

Kánvas and of the Mádhyandinas." The White Yajus in
the Mádhyandina recension is arranged into forty adhyáyas
or lectures, divided into three hundred and three anuvákas or sections, containing one thousand, nine hundred
and seventy-five kandíkás or portions. The last fifteen
adhyáyas of the White Yajus are of considerably later
origin;† and the last adhyáya is also regarded as an
Upanishad. And the redaction of the Yajus was ac-
complished by the Kurupanchálas and Kosala-Videhas
when they were in their prime.‡ The Black Yajus contains the formulas for the entire sacrificial ceremonial,
such as those to be found in the Samhitá of the White
Yajus; but the order in both of them is quite different.
The formulas, for the most part, are for the new and full-
moon sacrifices; for the morning and evening fire-sacrifices;
for the sacrifices to be offered every four months at the beginning of the three seasons; for the soma-sacrifice;
for the construction of altars; for the Sautrámani ceremony;
for the Asvamedha or horse-sacrifice; for the Purushamedha or human-sacrifice; for the Sarvamedha or universal sacrifice; for the Pitrimedha or oblation to the Manes;
and for the prayaçyya or purificatory sacrifice.

The Yajuh-Samhitá consists chiefly of prayers and invocations to be used at the consecration of utensils and at
sacrificial ceremonials. The origin of the Yajuh-Samhitá

* On the possible connexion of the Mádhyandinas with the Madiandi-
nes—see Weber's History of Indian Literature. p 106
† Ibid. p. 167.
‡ Ibid. pp. 24 ff.

was precisely due to circumstances like those of the
Sâman; but the paraphernalia of the equally complex
and highly developed ritual for which the compilation of
this Veda became absolutely necessary, is more elaborate
and more attractive than that of the Sâman. The Indo-
Aryans gave special preference to the Yajus; for it could
better satisfy their sacrificial wants than the Sâman or
the Rik. "The Yajur-veda," says Sâyana, in his Introduction to the Taittirîya-Samhitâ, "is like a wall, the
two other Vedas like fresco-paintings (on it)." The
history of the Yajuh-Samhitâ differs palpably enough
from that of the other Vedas; and such difference consists
in the disagreement between its own schools, which is far
more weighty than the dissensions which widened the
gulf between the schools of the other Vedas. These
schools were founded on a division of the Yajuh-Samhitâ;
the one party adhering to what is called the Black Yajus
and the other to the White Yajus. And there is strong
reason to suppose that this division must have taken place
even after the time of Pânini.[*] Some commentators explain sukla or 'white' by suddha.[†] The White Yajus is
attributed to Yâjnavalkya, and the Black Yajus to Tittiri.

   The Atharva-veda, though next to the Rik, is the
most comprehensive and valuable of the four collections.
The Atharvan is almost entirely a Rig-veda; but it has

[*] Goldstücker · Pânini. p. 130 ff.

[†] Thereby one explains शुक्ल इति by शुक्ल वा शुद्ध-
निविशेषणगुणवति ।

also many points of contact with the Yajus." And there
is no doubt that its songs rank chronologically with the
Brâhmanas of the Rik, the Sâman, and the Yajus. It
is more original than the last two; and consequently
more interesting. Though it repeats numerous hymns
of the Rig-veda, it contains a good many entirely now
ones. This is not exactly a Veda, although many of
the hymns or incantations of which it is composed,
appear to be of extreme antiquity.† It was but after a
hard struggle that the Atharvan came off victorious, and
at last took the rank as a fourth Veda.‡ The Atharvan,
however, not being used at the religious ceremonies,
and chiefly containing hymns to be used at lustrations,
appears to be altogether different from the other Vedas.
This Veda, upon the whole, belongs to the Brahmanical
period; and the songs and formulas aggregated into it also
properly belonged to the Vrâtyas or unbrahmanical
Aryans of the west.§ It is more like an historical than a
liturgical collection. The greater portion of the Atharvan
is borrowed from the last book of the Rik-Samhitâ.¶

* Weber's History of Indian Literature, p. 148.

† See, on the subject of this Veda, Müller's Ancient Sanskrit Literature,
pp. 38, 446 ff.; Weber's History of Indian Literature, p. 10; and Prof.
Whitney's papers in the Journal of the American Oriental Society, iii.
pp. 305 ff.; and iv. pp. 254 ff.

‡ Weber's History of Indian Literature, p. 11.

§ Ibid, p. 147.

¶ "By the followers of the Atharvan, the riches or stanzas of the Rig-
veda, are unanimously included in their own Samhitâ (or collection)."—
Sâyanâchârya, Introduction, Müller's edition, p. 2

I

The existing Samhitá belongs to the school of the Saunakas ; and to the period when Brahmanism had become
dominant. There was, however, another recension of the
Samhitá belonging to the Paippaláda school. But the
variations that occur in the text of the Saunakas are so
prominent that a learned writer calls them capricious
transpositions and alterations.* This collection appears
to consist of complete hymns, and not of single broken
and isolated verses ; and its internal arrangement is
authentic. In this respect it is akin to the Rik, and can
properly be called a complement of the first Veda, a complement containing a large mass of hymns essentially suited
to its time. This Veda is called after the name of Atharvan
or Atharva of the Zend-Avesta, where he is described as an
itinerant preacher or preceptor. The Atharva is divided into
twenty kándas or books ; of which the last two are said to be
supplementary. Of these books the first eighteen are arranged into thirty-four prapáthakas or chapters, which again
contain ninety-four anuvákas or sections ; the seventeenth
book consists of only one prapáthaka without any further
sub-division ; the nineteenth book is not arranged into prapáthakas, but simply into seven anuvákas ; and the twentieth
consists of only nine anuvákas, the third of which is made
up of three paryáyas. These anuvákas, upon the whole,
embrace about six thousand verses. This Veda, perhaps, on
account of the mystery which wraps up its songs, became, in
no small degree, invested with a halo of sacredness, which
surpassed even that of the older Vedas. From the A thar-

* Roth's Literature and History of the Veda, p. 12.

vanarahasya it appears that the other three Vedas enable a
man to fulfil the *dharma*, or religious law ; but the Atharvan helps him to attain *moksha*, or eternal beatitude.

The Atharva-Samhitâ is rather a supplement to the
Rig-veda than one of the four Vedas ; and has very little
coincidence with any of them in its general character.[*]
It marks off the period of transition from the simple faith
of the early times to the gross superstitions of the subsequent period. The Atharvan is not, however, so much
of priestly as of popular origin.[†] It was by all means
collected later than the Rik ; and despite the fact that it has
the grammatical forms of the older hymns its language
conclusively proves its later origin.[‡] Its most peculiar
feature consists not so much in the fact that it contains
matter quite of a distinctive character from that of the other
Vedas ; but as in the fact that it comprises a great number of
incantations. The Atharvan is not used for the sacrifice ; but
embraces formulas supposed to have the influence of protecting against injurious influences of the divine powers
and of the lunar asterisms too, with imprecations on enemies, prayers against diseases and noxious animals, as well
as for the efficacy of healing herbs, for protection in travel-
ling, luck in play, and such like things.[§] In general, the Atharvan is poor in its hymnological and liturgical portions.

---

* Wilson's Rig-veda, i. p. viii.
† Weber's History of Indian Literature, pp. 11, 167.
‡ Roth's Dissertation on the Atharva-veda, pp. 12, 17.
§ Roth's Literature and History of the Veda, p. 12 ; and Whitney's
Oriental and Linguistic Studies, pp. 20, L.

The first eighteen books of the Samhitâ, with which it was originally drawn up, are arranged upon one system throughout. A sixth of the bulk is not metrical; but consists of longer or shorter prose-pieces; which tally, in point of language and style, with the passages of the Brâhmanas. In the Atharva-veda the Bâhlîkas are mentioned (v. 22, 5, 7, 14); while the Rig-veda is quite ignorant of such people. At any rate the oldest Indians must have been acquainted with them. There is nothing of poetical conception in the Atharvan. It is rather full of sorcery and priestly vagaries and professions. There is also every mark of a complete development of ritual in it. It contains no hymn addressed to Vishnu, nor is there any hymn addressed to Indra such as we find in the Rik-Samhitâ. But there is a hymn dedicated to Varuna which is remarkable in every respect. This hymn formed an oath to be taken by a witness (iv. 16—comp. z. 5, 36, 44; xvi. 7, 8; xvi. 8, 1). Though there are indications of a full-blown polytheism in the Atharvan; yet there are also some traces to be found of a progress towards monotheism. As regards the authorship tradition does not afford any valuable information; but the hymns with some exceptions, are ascribed to fictitious personages. The contents of the Atharvan are a medley; but there is to be found in some books some uniformity in the subject-matter. The fourteenth book deals with marriage; the fifteenth with the glorification of Vrâtya; the sixteenth as well as the seventeenth with omens and portents; and the eighteenth with burial and the Manes-sacrifice.

The Vedas do not appear to be the productions of one

and the same author or even of the same age." "At
whatever time the work may have been performed, it constituted a decided era in the literary history of India. Thence-
forth the texts became a chief object of the science and
industry of the nation, as their contents had always attrac-

* It seems strange that one so well informed as Max Müller should have
published the following lines. "In the most ancient Sanskrit literature,
the idea even of authorship is excluded. Works are spoken of as revealed
to and communicated by certain sages, but not as composed by them."
History of Ancient Sanskrit Literature, p. 556. The earlier Rishis did not in
any case lay claim to inspiration nor did they look upon their compositions as
divinely inspired, but they knew and believed themselves simply to be
the authors of the hymns of the Veda, and not to be writing by inspiration
from God, as it has been alleged since they frequently speak of them as the
productions of their own minds. They appear to have distinctly described
themselves as the composers of the hymns. The verbs which they employ
to express this idea are *kri*, "to make" (i. 104, 6 ; ii. 35, 2 ; iii. 39, 2 ; iv. 6, 11 ,
vi. 32, 1 ; vii. 35, 14 ; viii. 51, 4 , ix. 73, 2 ; x. 54, 6 ; x. 191, 2) , *takṣ*, "to
fabricate", the literal equivalent i. 62, 13 ; i. 130, 6 ; ii. 19, 8 , iii. 65, 4,
v. 2, 11 ; v. 29, 15 ; vi. 32, 1 , vii. 7, 6. viii. 6, 33 , x. 39, 14 , x. 80, 7) , and
jan "to beget," or "produce" (ix. 2, 1 ; vii. 15, 4 , viii. 32, 9 , viii. 43, 2 ; viii.
77, 6 ; viii. 84, 4, 5 ; ix. 73, 2 ; x. 67, 1) Nevertheless the Rishis were not
altogether unconscious of higher influences (iii. 57, 4) ; and they seem to have
attached a high value to their productions, which, as they believed, were
acceptable to the gods (v. 44, 4 ; v. 85, 1 ; vii. 33, 1, 2 ; x. 23, 6 , x. 54, 4 ;
x. 105, 8). There are also a great multitude of passages in the Rik which
ascribe a supernatural character to the earlier Rishis (vii. 76, 4 ; iii. 53, 9 ;
vii. 33, 11 ff ; vii. 87. 4 ; vii. 88, 3 ff ; x. 14, 15 ; x. 62, 4, 5) ; and even to the
hymns (i. 77, 4 iii. 18, 3 ; vii. 34, 1 , vii. 34, 9 , x. 176, 2). There are similar
passages to be met with in Homer and Hesiod. The Rishis are said to have
held intercourse about sacred truths with the gods (i. 179, 2 ; vii. 76, 4)
Again, on the other hand, some among them professed their ignorance of all
matters either human or divine (i. 164, 5). There are many hymns in which
it appears also that the consciousness of some affinity with the divine nature
was uppermost in their mind ; and they likewise believed to have been a re-

ted its highest reverence and admiration ; and so thorough
and religious was the care bestowed upon their preservation, that, notwithstanding their mass and the thousands of

dowed with superior wisdom, and to have possessed the knowledge of the
deities. ii. 21, 1 ; iii. 23, 3 ; v. 29, 1 . vi. 14, 3 , viii. 6, 61 ; ix. 107, 7 ; x. 112,
5. When the like book of inspiration and of independent composition is
at the same time traceable in the Rik-Sanhitá, it is possible that the action
of inspiration may not have occupied the minds of the earlier sages ; but may
have grown up among their successors, or more properly that it may have
been entertained by some and not by all of them. The Rishis sought from their
gods every kind of temporal blessings, such as long life, food, riches, strength,
offspring, cattle and rain. And they in like manner expressed that those
gods would direct their devotional acts, stimulate their poetical powers, and
inspire them to compose hymns in honor of them. Hence we can also find
distinct indications in some of the hymns of superhuman character ascribed
to the Rishis themselves, and of divine influence which suggested their compositions (Müir's Sanskrit Texts, iii. p. ...). But when the Vedas suffered
into inspired compositions we are not now in a position to say even approxi-
mately. The claims as to the divine and infallible character of the Vedas must
have been set up gradually. But a protest seems to have been made by the
Buddhists against such claims during the ... period (compare Yáska's
Nirukta, i. 15). And it is also mentioned that the reverence for the Veda must
have been as the same before the days of Yáska and Pánini (Pánini. iv. 4, 63).
The Indian authors shortly before, or subsequent to, the collection of the
Vaidik writings hold the opinions on the origin of the Vedas as springing
from the mystical sacrifice of Purusha, Rig-veda, x. 90, 9 ; as resting on
Skambha, Atharva-veda, x. 7, 14 , as springing from Indra, xiii. 4, 34 ; as
produced from time, xix. 54, 3 ; as produced from Agni, Váyu, and Súrya,
Manu, i. 21-23, and Satapatha-Bráhmana, xi 5. 8. 1 ff. ; as springing from
Prajápati, and the waters, Satapatha-Bráhmana, vi 1, 1, 8 ; as springing
from the ... of the sacrifice (mahábhúta), Atharva-veda, xi 7, 24 , as
issued from the mouth of Brahmá at the creation. Vishnu-Purána, i. 6, 48 ff.,
Bhágavata-Purána, iii 12, 34 and 37 ff., and Márkandeya-Purána, 102, 1 ;
as created by Brahmá or as produced from the Gáyatrí. Harivansa, verses
47, and 11,516 ; as created by Vishnu, or as having Sarasvatí for their

years which have elapsed since their collection, hardly a
single various reading, so far as is yet known, has been
suffered to make its way into them after their definite and
final establishment. The influence which they have exer-
ted upon the whole literary development of after ages is
not easily to be rated too high."*

All that is not found of the oldest Veda in the Sáman
and the Yajus, is a Rik piece-meal; its hymns broken into
parts; verses from different hymns assembled anew; and
even the composition of numerous parts aggregated into
the same songs, as if they had the same author. That
under such circumstances, the Yajus should have lost its
interest so far as poetry is concerned, was only to be expected; it is, however, a curious fact, that the Sáman
has preserved so much of that beauty which so peculiarly
marks the Rig-veda poetry. The Atharvan, too, is composed in like manner as the Yajus, with only some variants,
so that the additions in it to the mutilated extracts from
the Rik, are more considerable than those in the Yajus.

There exists no record that carries us back to a more

mother, Mahábhárata, Sánipurva, verse 12,969; and a passage in the
Taittiríya-Bráhmana speaks of the Veda as being "the hair of Prajápati's
beard." iii. 39, 1, etc., etc.   In like manner, many other authorities might be
cited to the same effect; but they are also puerile and contradictory
in themselves.   The Rishis designated the older hymns, and the more
recent ones by various names, such as arka, uktha, rich, gir, slok, súktha, nivid,
mantra, mati, stoma, stoma, stiel, vachas, ahvan, gaha, samansa, navichit,
manti, dhíti, dhishana, stuti, svara, mantari, pranati, etc. etc.; and they
also often applied to them the title of brahma which has also the sense of
hymn or prayer (iv. 14, 21; v. 29, 15; vi. 17, 15; vi. 54, 6; vii. 61, 6, 2.
60, 3).

* Whitney's Oriental and Linguistic Studies, p. 32.

primitive state of the human family than the *Rig-veda*. And the few relics that have been preserved to us, are of most intense interest. It has been very appropriately said that there is one oasis in the vast desert of ancient Asiatic history, and it is the only real Veda, the *Rig-veda*, the earliest existing literary record of the whole Aryan race.[*] The priority of the *Rik* to all the other Vedas is thoroughly established by the fact that its numerous hymns are repeated in them; and that its *Rishis* are referred to even in the Atharvan. But in the Atharvan the names of the *Rishis* thus produced, are principally of the more recent *Rishis*; while those in the *Rik* are of the greatest antiquity.[†] In the Atharvan a more developed state of the institutions together with the caste system appears than what we find in the *Rik*. In the former we see the people bound hand and foot by the fetters of a wily and tyrannical hierarchy and superstition; while in the latter we find them quite free, and imbued with a warm love of nature. Judging from the language and internal character of the Atharvan, we arrive at the conclusion that the main body of this Veda was in existence at a time when the *Rik* was compiled. In the White Yajush Samhitâ an enumeration is given of the different classes of men who are to be consecrated at the Purushamedha, and of the means of most of the mixed castes. We may, therefore, conclude that the Brahmanical element had then gained the supremacy, and the system of caste was completely organised.[‡]

[*] Müller's Chips from a German Workshop i. p. 5.
[†] Roth's Literature and History of the Veda. p. 13.
[‡] Weber's History of Indian Literature p. 111.

The 90th hymn of the tenth book of the *Rig-veda* is entitled the Purusha-sûkta ; which also occurs in the 31st book of the Vâjasaneyi-Samhitâ (1-16), and in the 19th book of the Atharva-veda (6, 1ff.) There it is said that the Brahman, Kshattriya, Vaisya did not issue respectively from the mouth, arms, and thighs of Purusha ; but simply the Brahman was his mouth, the Râjasya was made his arms, the Vaisya was his thighs, and the Sûdra only sprang from his feet.° The text thus conclusively proves that there was no caste ; but there were only four different classes of people. The fact that the Sâman has not extracted any verse from it, is not without meaning.† The opening parts of the Sûkta are of a pantheistic character ; and the whole of it contains allusions to the sacrificial ceremonials, and not to the actual immolation of a human victim. In it, the sacrifice is not offered to the gods but by the gods themselves. Nor are there human priests mentioned ; and the Purusha could not have been an ordinary man. It is full of technical and philosophical terms ; and contains certain modern words such as Sûdra, Râjasya Vaisya, Sâdhyas and prishadâjya; and there is also mention made of the three seasons—spring, summer and autumn, which do not occur in any other hymn. A reference is also made to the four different kinds of Vaidik compositions such as rik, sâman, chhandas, and yajus, which distinctly proves the comparatively later date of the Sûkta. And, no doubt, here the Atharvas is referred to under the appellation of *Chhandas.* From these facts it is apparent that

° Mahâbhârata. iii. 12.961.

† Weber's Indische Studien, ix. p. 2.

It belongs to the close of the Vaidik age; and it is also found scarcely to enunciate any uniform, orthodox and authoritative doctrine in regard to the four-fold origin of the human race.[*]

The various hymns of the Rik-Sanhitá were composed by various Rishis. Each hymn is said to have had its Rishi; and these Rishis comprise a variety of secular as well as religious individuals, who became famous at different times in Indian tradition. The primitive traditions, though few, are yet sufficient to prove that in the Vaidik age the capacity for metrical composition, and the highest prerogative of officiating at the worship of the gods, were not regarded as exclusively confined to individuals of priestly caste. Even females are spoken of as authors of hymns or parts of hymns, as Romasá, daughter of Brihaspati (I. 126), Lopámudrá (I. 179, 1), and Viśvavárá, of the family of Atri (v. 28). And it is also a very remarkable and curious fact that we find one Kavasha Ailúsha, himself a Śúdra,[†] to have composed a few of the Súktas in the tenth book of the Rig-veda. The epithets applied by the authors of the hymns to themselves and to the sages who in earlier times had appointed, as well as to their contemporaries who followed them in conducting, the different rites at the worship of the gods, are the following: rishi, kavi, medhátithi, vipra, vipaschit, vedhas, muni, etc. The Vedas are said to have been perpetuated by oral tradition, until they were collected and arranged by a school or

[*] Muir's Original Sanskrit Texts, I. pp. 7-15; Colebrooke's Essays i. p. 309, note; Müller's History of Ancient Sanskrit Literature, pp. 570, f.
[†] Aitareya-Bráhmana, ii. 19; Kaushitaki-Bráhmana, xi.

schools of learned Brahmans of which the nominal head was
Krishna Dvaipāyana Vyāsa, the Indian Pisistratus.* Vyāsa,
who flourished in the early part of the twelfth century
B. C.,† having collected and arranged with others the so-
called revealed scriptures, taught them to some of his
disciples, viz., the Rik to Paila, the Yajus to Vaisampāyana,
the Sāman to Jaimini, and the Atharvan to Sumantu ;
and they in like manner taught to their disciples, who
again in their turn communicated their knowledge to their
pupils.‡

The Vedas are written in an ancient form of Sanskrit ;
which is to the later what Chaucer's writings are to
modern English. They abound in obsolete and peculiar
expressions made up of the more recent grammatical forms
with such irregularity as leads to the inference that the
language was too unsettled and variable to be brought
under subjection to a system of rigid grammatical rules.

The Vaidik dialect is to be understood as the least altered representative of that original tongue from which are
descended the languages of the leading races of Asia and
Europe. The dialect of the first three Vedas is very
ancient and at the same time very difficult. When it is
compared with the classical Sanskrit it appears that both

* Lassen's Indian Antiquities, I. p. 777, note ; and also Mahābhārata,
I. 3417 and 4236.

† Archdeacon Pratt's Letter on Colebrooke's Determination of the Date
of the Veda in the Journal of the Asiatic Society of Bengal, 1862, vol. xxxi.
pp. 49 sq.; and Journal of the American Oriental Society, viii. pp. 82.

‡ Weber's Vājasaneyi-Samhitā, p. 1 . Colebrooke's Essays, i. p. 11 ;
and Wilson's Rig veda, i. p. 22.

are phonetically and grammatically very far from being the
same, and lexically they are as wide as possible. "The language of the Vedas is an older dialect, varying very considerably, both in its grammatical and lexical character, from
the classical Sanskrit. Its grammatical peculiarities run
through all departments : euphonic rules, word-formation
and composition, declension, conjugation, syntax. . . . .
[These peculiarities] are partly such as characterise an
older language, consisting in a greater originality of forms,
and the like, and partly such as characterise a language
which is still in the bloom and vigour of life, its freedom
untrammelled by other rules than those of common usage,
and which has not, like the (classical) Sanskrit, passed into
oblivion as a native spoken dialect, because merely a con-
ventional medium of communication among the learned,
being forced, as it were, into a mould of regularity by
long and exhausting grammatical treatment. . . . . . .
The dissimilarity existing between the two, in respect of
the stock of words of which each is made up, is, to say the
least, not less marked. Not single words alone, but whole
classes of derivations and roots, with the families that are
formed from them, which the Veda exhibits in frequent
and familiar use, are wholly wanting, or have left but
faint traces, in the classical dialect ; and this to such an
extent as seems to demand, if the two be actually related
to one another directly as mother and daughter, a longer
interval between them than we should be inclined to
assume, from the character and degree of the grammatical,
and more especially the phonetic, differences.""

* Journal of the American Oriental Society, iii. pp. 296, ff.

The chronology of the Vaidik age is indicated in the different styles of composition which are to be met with in the Vedas as well as in the Brâhmanas and the Sûtras. The Vaidik age is divided by Müller into four distinct periods : namely, the Chhandas period, the Mantra period, the Brâhmana period, and the Sûtra period. The respective styles of composition of these four periods seem to differ very much from one another. In the Chhandas period the oldest hymns were composed ; and this period in fact furnishes us with a fair picture of the primitive society of the Indo-Aryans at a time when no particular system of religion was prevalent. Even sacrifices were not then in vogue. But in the Mantra period they came to be held in great estimation ; and in this period the more recent hymns were composed, and the whole was placed together and arranged into one Samhitâ. Three other Samhitâs were also collected and arranged systematically for a distinct theological or sacrificial purpose. At this time there were priests by profession, who had elaborated a most highly complex system of sacrifices. In the Brâhmana period the principal theological and liturgical books bearing this title were composed and marshalled together ; and theological speculations were much indulged in. In the Sûtra period the ceremonial precepts of the earlier times were reduced to a systematic form. The works of this period were not all written in the enigmatical form of Sûtras, but some were in verse and others in prose. The Vedas have their own Brâhmanas and Sûtras : and as the Sûtras presuppose the Brâhmanas, and the Brâhmanas do not refer to them, it is proved that

5

the Brâhmana period must have preceded the Sûtra period. In the Brâhmana and Sûtra periods the Sanskrit language must have undergone considerable modifications. The Sûtra period extends far into the Buddhistic times ; and we can place this period on the frontier of the Vaidik age. In this period certainly occurred one of the most remarkable changes in the Indo-Aryan religion and society.

The Chhandas period may be supposed, according to Max Müller, to have lasted from 1800 to 1000 B. C. ; the Mantra period from 1000 to 800 B. C. ; the Brâhmana period from 800 to 600 B. C. ; and the Sûtra period from 600 to 200 B. C. "To decide the question," says Barthélémy Saint-Hilaire, "with absolute certainty as to the dates of these four periods of ancient Sanskrit literature, would be impossible ; for Indian literature itself is almost without known dates, owing either to the peculiar organisation of the Hindu mind, or to the convulsions of Indian society. The present condition of Sanskrit philology does not afford the scholar the requisite data for embarking with any chance of success in such chronological speculations. Uncertainty hangs over these periods ; and to assign an approximate length to each of these periods is altogether hazardous. It should be well understood that these dates are only approximately accurate ; and notwithstanding the apparent accuracy of the figures, it is clear that one cannot in this case arrive at any precise conclusion. Moreover, Max Müller would perhaps have done better, if he had not sought to fix such precise limits to write down the result of his investigations so accurately. As there is necessarily always much vagueness in calcu-

lations of this nature, it is well that the form given to hypo-
theses be just as vague as our data ; and as there is nothing
so certain as a number once pronounced, I think it would
have been better to remain partly in the dark, which in
fact, is quite excusable in such matters. Besides, every
body will see that the chronological limits assigned by
Max Müller to the four periods of Vaidik literature are too
narrow rather than too wide. The same conviction has
been expressed by Professor Wilson and Dr. Whitney.
If Max Müller is wanting in any thing it is chiefly
through an excess of reserve. The period of the Samhitâs,
such as we now possess, is dated at least 1000 years before
the Christian era. One may, without the slightest hesita-
tion, place the period of the Chhandas far beyond that.
Then again one alights upon the calculations of Sir William
Jones, and of Colebrooke, who assigned to the composition
of the *Rig*-veda a period fourteen or fifteen hundred
years before Christ.

In another point of view, this uniform length of two
centuries assigned to the period of the Brâhmanas, as well
as to that of the Mantras and of the Chhandas, is equally
open to criticism. If the period of the Sûtras comprised
four entire centuries, it seems hardly probable that the
period of the Brâhmanas which are quite as long, and perhaps equally numerous, should not have extended over
a longer time, including the A'ranyakas and the Upanishads. Moreover there is certainly a far smaller interval
between the Brâhmanas and the Sûtras, than there is between the Mantras and the Brâhmanas. Nevertheless Max
Müller reckons only two centuries between each of these

two periods. Analogy would seem to authorize the assumption of a far longer interval between the latter two than between the former two. There is an immense difference between the period assigned to the collection of sacred poetry, and the period in which they are commented upon ; there is a smaller difference between this latter epoch and the one in which these manifold and obscure commentaries are reduced to clear and orderly rules. As for the period of the Mantras, it seems in its turn too extensive, if that of the Brâhmaṇas is not sufficiently so. Granted that two centuries had been necessary for the composition of the Brâhmaṇas, the simple collection of the Saṃhitâs did not require so much time. Thus, without contesting the absolute length of the united periods, their relative lengths do not seem to be very acceptable, and their proportions might be settled in a totally different manner, which could be equally justified. As for the period of the Chhandas, the first of all, and the most fertile, since it has rendered all the rest comparatively worthless, it is to be presumed that it was the longest ; and this inspiration, which, during more than three thousand years, has enlivened the entire religious creed of a great people, cannot have been of so short a duration, since its effects are so durable."

First of all were composed the hymns, and then the Brâhmaṇas. It is, therefore, possible that several centuries intervened between the composition of both the hymns and the Brâhmaṇas, as a not inconsiderable space of time must have been required for the literal meaning and purport of the hymns becoming somewhat obscure and doubtful, and invested with a halo of sacredness. In the same manner

the period during which the Brâhmanas were drawn up
must have been separated from that of the Sûtras by
several centuries, as a sufficient space of time must have
elapsed for farther modification of language, and the
growth of a new theology which claimed for the Brâhmanas the same sacredness which the Brâhmanas themselves did for the hymns. There are however no sufficient
data by which we can determine with precision the period
during which the hymns were composed. The hymns
are divided into two classes, the Mantras or more recent hymns which according to some scholars may have
been produced between 1000 and 800 years before the
Christian era ; and the Chhandas or the older hymns
which, they suppose, may have been composed between
1200 and 1000 B. C. Other scholars hold altogether a
different opinion ;* and it is shared by Dr. Haug who
writes thus : "We do not hesitate, therefore, to assign
the composition of the bulk of the Brâhmanas to the
years 1400-1200 B. C. ; for the Sambitâ we require a
period of at least 500-600 years, with an interval of
about two hundred years between the end of the proper
Brâhmana period. Thus we obtain for the bulk of Sambitâ
the space from 1400-2000 ; the oldest hymns and sacrificial formulas may be a few hundred years more ancient
still, so that we would fix the very commencement of
Vaidik literature between 2000-2400 B. C."† The chronological distance of the Vaidik age is to be measured not

* Müller's Ancient Sanskrit Literature, p. 572 ; and his edition of the
Rig-veda, iv. pp. iv.-xiii.

† Haug's Aitareya-Brâhmana, i. p. 47.

merely by the revolutions and progress of the heavenly bodies ; but also by the revolutions and progress of the human mind. We do not see any reason why there should be altogether a distinct era for the Chhandas when it may be held as the same with the Mantra period which undoubtedly included the new, intermediate and ancient hymns.* However, there are no mile-stones in Vaidik literature. The classification of ancient Sanskrit literature has now become a theme for discussion by every Sanskrit scholar. But where it is to end is not easy to surmise. It has been questioned whether the basis of that classification is scientific or ritual or theological. But whatever may be advanced against such an arrangement, we have every reason to place our faith in the distribution of Vaidik literature into distinct periods.

* Wilson's Works, v. p. 697 ; Roer's Aitareya-Brāhmana, I. p. 23 ; and Goldstucker's Pāṇini, p. 71.

———

CHAPTER IV.

*The Division of the Vedas into Mantras and Bráhmanas—
the proper meaning of Sákhá, Charana, and
Parishad—the Áranyakas—the Upanishads—
and the Distinction between Sruti and
Smriti.*

THE division of the Vedas is two-fold, Mantras and
Bráhmanas.[*] Such a division is indeed an essential one:
especially when it separates two different classes of writings,
which are related to one another as canonized text on the
one hand, and canonised explanation on the other. That
part of each Veda which contains the mantras—the metrical
hymns or prose forms of prayer, is called its Samhitá ; and
this definition applies equally to all the Samhitás except
that of the Black Yajur Veda, in which both the
Mantra and the Bráhmana portions are combined. But
yet it is to be believed that this Samhitá had a separate

[*] Sáyana says in his commentary on the Rig-veda : "The definition (of
the Veda) as a book composed of mantra and bráhmana, is unobjectionable
Hence Ápastamba says in the Yajna-paribháshá, 'Mantra and Bráhmana
have the name of Veda.' "

Brāhmaṇa annexed to it.* The Brāhmaṇas stand to the
Mantras in the same relation as the Talmud does to the
Mosaic code. The former presuppose the earlier existence
of the latter ; and the proof that the Mantras are far older
than any other portion of Indian literature, is to be found
particularly in the character of their language. Though
the Mantras and the Brāhmaṇas were held at a later period
to have existed together, it admits of no question that the
Brāhmaṇa portion of each Veda is posterior at least to
some part of its Saṃhitā ; for the former evidently refers
to, and contains extracts from the latter.† And it needs
scarcely be stated that so large a collection of works including both the portions must have been the gradual product of
several centuries. Indeed, they represent various mutations
of society, various phases of religious belief, and even different periods of language. The difficulty in distinguishing
these periods is however immensely increased by the apparent losses, which these writings must have sustained before
they were aggregated together and preserved in the shape
in which we now find them. The Mantras and the Brāhmaṇas had to pass through a large number of Sākhās ;

* Müller's History of Ancient Sanskrit Literature, p. 360 ; and Weber's
History of Indian Literature, p. 62.

† On the subject of the priority of the hymns to the Brāhmaṇas the
commentator of the Taittīrya, or Black Yajur-veda, Raibhila, thus delivers
himself :—"Although the Veda is formed both of Mantra and Brāhmaṇa,
yet as the Brāhmaṇa consists of an explanation of the Mantras, it is the
latter which were at first recorded" (p. 9 of the Calcutta edition). Sáyaṇa
in his commentary on the Brāhma-Āraṇyaka Upanishad also says that "the
Mantras are the source of the Brāhmaṇas."—Müller's Ancient India, ii. pp.
353, &c.

and consequently the dissensions, which sprang up among
those schools, either in connexion with the Vaidik texts or
their interpretations were very bitter. The Mantras are
generally in verse, whilst the Brāhmaṇas are entirely in
prose. The Mantras, in fact, were for ages unwritten,
and the elliptical style of their composition is the only
evidence of their oral transmission.

Most of the Brāhmaṇas are collective works ; and there
are old and new Brāhmaṇas. But those that have now
perished, are found in diverse manner quoted or referred to.
They were, in fact, the productions of the schools of the
Brahmanic priesthood. Though they are puerile, and in
the main tediously prolix, verbose and artificial, yet they
are found to contain much important matter both theological and ceremonial. We also find in them the oldest
rituals, the oldest linguistic expositions, the oldest legendary narratives, and the oldest philosophical and mythical
speculations all of which are mixed up with each other.
But they seem to differ widely from one another in point
of details ; and this is simply owing to the fact that they
belong to one or the other of the Vedas. With respect to
their origin and age they occupy a kind of intermediate
position between the transition from a simple Vaidik mode
of thought to the Brahmanical vagaries.* And this
transition was indeed brought about solely by the Brāhmaṇas themselves. They were drawn up with a view to en-
force various ceremonies and sacrifices, to illustrate the
use of the hymns at them, and to enjoin the duties of the

* Weber's History of Indian Literature, p 12.

different classes of priests. The authors, however, generally failed to understand the rational meaning of the
hymns, and so suggested the most absurd explanations of
the various formularies which of course had originally
some reasonable drift. The number of the old Brâhmanas
must have been very considerable as every Sâkhâ consisted of a Samhitâ and a Brâhmana. It must not, therefore,
be supposed that the Brâhmanas were not all composed
independently by different authors. Each Brâhmana is
included in its own Veda, and is ascribed to no human
author. The different Brâhmanas in fact obtained their
names from the schools by which they were transmitted.
For the Rig-veda we have the Aitareya, and the Sânkhâyana or Kaushitaki ; for the Sâma-veda, the Praudha, the
Shadvinsa, the Sâmavidhi, etc ; for the White Yajur-veda
the Satapatha; for the Black Yajur-veda the Taittirîya ;
and for the Atharva-veda the Gopatha. The Brâhmanas of
the Rik generally prescribe the duties of the Hotris. The
Brâhmanas of the Sâman specify the duties of the Udgâtris; and the Brâhmanas of the Yajus confine themselves
to the duties of the Adhvaryus.

A Brâhmana was originally a theological tract, and it
was so designated because it owed its origin to *brahman* or
prayer." The entire collection of Brâhmanas gives also
impression of having undergone a secondary alteration ;

<hr/>

" Instead of saying the same over again, we quote the following words of
Haug. —The word brahma or brahman is the most important word in
Hindu theology and philosophy. Brahma comes now in the Rigveda-
or the Sâmi, as a name for "soul" (Anamisma 2. 7), and for "prayer"
(Rhamudina 2, 10). In Sâyana's commentary on the hymns of the Rig-veda
it is sometimes explained with reference to this signification, and sometimes

and their prevalence constitutes a distinct stage in the
progress of the religious history of the Indo-Aryans. As
the dogmatical books of the Brahmans they contain a
system of tenets, which were of necessity the result of religious practice. If they do not afford a rational explanation
of the principles of belief, they are still very useful for such
an exposition, because they were composed with the distinct
object of explaining and establishing the whole sacrificial

in other ways, on. gr., (1) food, in general, 1, 16, 4 ; more frequently, sacrificial food as in 6, 32, 1 ; (2) performance of the song of the Soma singers, 7,
33, 7 ; (3) magic, charm, spell, 2, 32, 3 ; (4) ceremonies, having a song of praise
as their characteristic ; (5) performance of song and sacrifice 7, 32, 1 ; (6)
the recitation of the Hotri priests ; (7) grace, 6, 32, 1. These all seem to
point to the principal meanings, namely, "food," in particular "sacrificial
food," and the performance of the song at the sacrifice. The meaning
"devotion" given to the word "brahma" is quite inapplicable. In the language
of the Avesta we find, so far as could be ascertained, an absolutely identical word, namely baresma. By it the Pârsis understand a regularly
cut bundle of twigs tied together with grass, and used at their Fire-ceremo-
nies exactly as the little clipped bundle of kusa grass is used by Brahmans,
at the Soma sacrifices. This latter is called Veda (A'svalâyana, Srauta-Sutra,
1,11) which passes later as a synonym of brahma. This bunch of grass as
well as the baresma has a symbolical meaning. They both represent growing harvests, prosperity. The original meaning of the word was growth.
Hence came the meaning "prosperity," "success." As the success of the sacrifice entirely depended upon the holy texts, the chanting, the sacrificial
forms and offerings, the word could be used for any one of these essentials.
As the chanting of the hymns of praise was the most important of these
the word was most frequently employed in this sense. As sacrifice with the
Vedic Indian was the chief means to obtain all earthly and spiritual
blessings, but was itself useless without the brahma i. e. success, the latter
was at last regarded as the original cause of all beings. —Haug, Brahma und
die Brahmanen, p. 68 : Muir's Original Sanskrit Texts, I. pp. 240-65.

ceremonial. They exhibit, upon the whole, a distinct phase
in the intellectual history of the Indo-Aryans ; but in a
literary point of view, they are altogether without any
interest. They are in the main marked by sober reasoning,
full of genuine thoughts, lofty expressions, and valuable
traditions ; but their general characteristics mainly consist
in their archaisms, grammatical irregularities, antiquated
and tautological style and antiquarian pedantry. In them
we find a pantheistic system ; and this system was adopted simply for the explanation of the Vaidik deities. There
also occur numerous tales of the battles between the Devas
and the Asuras, which are to be understood as traditional
reminiscences of the hostilities between the Indo-Aryans
and the Assyrians during their wanderings in Asia before
the Indian immigration. Even there the Brahman, the
Kshattriya, the Vaisya, and the Sudra are repeatedly
named by their proper appellations ; and their peculiar
offices and relative stations are also clearly discriminated.

The Gopatha-Brahmana of the Atharva-veda is the
Veda of the Bhrigu-angiras ; which does not properly
belong to the sacred literature of the Indo-Aryans. This
Brahmana is of a small size. Its language is similar to
that of the other Brahmanas. Nothing is treated of in it in
all its details ; and even the manner in which every topic
is discussed is by no means interesting. The primary
object of this Brahmana is to show and establish the
importance and also the efficacy of the four Vedas. The
Purvardha, or the first part of it, comprises five prapāthakas ; and the other part, called the Uttarardha, consists
of six prapāthakas. The customary ceremonial of wor-

ship is discussed in it in like manner as in the other Bráhmanas; and there is, indeed, very little difference to be
seen between the Gopatha and those Bráhmanas.   It
begins with a theory of the creation of the universe as
do the other Bráhmanas.   It deals with the importance of áchamana, the rules regarding díkshá, the
mystic connexion of the year with ceremonies,   the
creation and requirements of ceremonies, the morning,
noon, and evening rites and other minor sacrifices.   It is
also remarkable on account of the chapter of accidents.
It was composed after the schism of the Charakas and the
Vájasaneyins* and the completion of the Vájasaneyi-
Samhitá ; and we must at any rate assign to it a later
date than to the Bráhmanas of the other Vedas.   It was
written probably about six centuries B. C.   The number of
Bráhmanas belonging to the Sáma-veda, is eight ; and
their names are : the Prauḍha or Mahá-Bráhmana (i.e., the
Tándya or Panchavinsa) the Shadvinsa, the Sámavidhi, the
A'rsheya, the Devatádhyáya, the Vansa, the Samhitopani-
shad, and the Upanishad,† which probably is the Chhándogya-Upanishad, and is thus ranked among the Bráhmanas.‡   The A'rsheya-Bráhmana is an Anukramaní consisting of three and a half prapáthakas.   It is found in both
the recensions of the Kauthumas and the Jaiminíyas ; but
the latter differs considerably from the former. This Bráhmana is devoted to an enumeration of the Seers of the

* Müller's History of Ancient Sanskrit Literature, pp. 451, ff; and see
also Mitra's Gopatha-Bráhmana, pp. 11-37.

† Müller's History of Ancient Sanskrit Literature, p. 348.

‡ Müller's Rig-veda, i. p. xxvii

L

Sáman. The Devatádhyáya is composed of four khandas. It embraces some miscellaneous fragments both old and new; but has no literary value. This Bráhmana contains philological speculations regarding the names of some Vaidik metres, and also shows some traces of the Buddhist influences. The Vansa is full of myths and legends of great value. This Bráhmana is also called an Anukramani; and it is similar in character to the A'rsheya. The Tándya-Bráhmana, also called the Panchavinsa, contains twenty-five books; and treats chiefly of Soma sacrifice. It contains also minute descriptions of the sacrifices performed on the banks of the Saraswati and Drishadvati; and of the Vrátyastomas or sacrifices by which such Aryans as were against Brahmanical polity, had admission to the Brahman community. This Bráhmana is also extremely rich in legendary contents as well as in information of a general nature; but; upon the whole, its contents are very dry. It was contemporary with, or even anterior to the flourishing epoch of the kingdom of the Kurupanchálas.[*] The Shadvinsa-Bráhmana, which is a supplement to the Panchavinsa, treats of expiatory sacrifices and imprecatory ceremonies. It is supposed to be of very modern date. And it not only alludes to temples but also to the images of the gods. The Samavidhi is in three chapters; and is of a highly artificial character, and presents no feature of interest. It appears that this Bráhmana has undergone some rearrangement, and belongs to a movement which resulted in the philosophies of Kumárila and Sankara. The subject-matter is nothing else than

---

[*] Weber's History of Indian Literature, p. 68.

the description of certain penances and ceremonies which
are altogether of little value. There is, however, mention
made of ceremonies some of which are meant for the expiation of sins and crimes ; and in fact there was then no
distinction between them.* We are therefore warranted to
conclude that it contains the germs of the criminal law
of later times.† Burnell assigns to this Brâhmana in its
present form not a higher antiquity than the 6th century
B. C.‡ A later Brâhmana probably of modern date, and
which is not mentioned by Sâyana, is the Adbhuta-Brâh-
mana. It treats of evil occurrence of daily life, omens
and portents.

The Chhândogya-Brâhmana of the Sâma-veda, of which
the Chhândogya-Upanishad constitutes a part, comprises
ten prapâthakas ; of these the first two are called the
Chhândogya-mantra-Brâhmana, and the rest forms the
Chhândogya-Upanishad. Of the two chapters of the
Chhândogya-Brâhmana the first embraces eight sûktas
on the ceremony of marriage, and the ceremonies to be
performed at the birth of a child. The second chapter
includes eight sûktas, which are consecrated to the Earth,
Agni, and Indra. It also contains mantras for offering
oblations to the Manes, Sûrya, and various other
deities very often united with a prayer for wealth, health,
and prosperity. The concluding mantra has reference to
the marriage ceremony. This Brâhmana contains also
a mass of highly interesting legends indicating the gradual

* Maine's Ancient Law, p. 371.
† Burnell's Sâmavidhâna, p. xvi.
‡ Ibid, p. x.

development of Brahmanic theology. The Aitareya-Brahmana originated in the country of the Kurupanchálas and Vasa-Usinarpa. This Bráhmana is one of the collections of the sayings of ancient Brahmá priests explanatory of the sacred duties of the so-called Hotri priests. Its style is throughout uniform. The greater part of the work appears to have been written by one and the same author; some additions, however, were made afterwards. This Brahmana and the Sánkháyana or Kaushitaki-Bráhmana are closely connected with each other; but there are points of divergence in the distribution of their matter. Though they treat essentially of the same matter, their views of the same question often appear to be antagonistic. The Aitareya contains eight panchikas or pentades, divided into forty adhyáyas or lectures, which again are sub-divided into 285 khandas or portions; but the last ten adhyáyas are but a later addition to it. This work treats chiefly of Soma sacrifice. The Sánkháyana is a perfectly arranged work, and consists of thirty adhyáyas, likewise sub-divided into a number of khandas. It embraces the complete sacrificial procedure. This Bráhmana originated simultaneously with the last few books of the Sambitá of the White Yajus. It also appears that the first thirty adhyáyas of the Aitareya-Bráhmana are older than those of the Sánkháyana.*

The Satapatha-Bráhmana, according to the Mádhyamdina school, is divided into 14 kándas or books, which contain 100 adhyáyas or lectures; or into 68 prapáthakas, with 438 bráhmanas, and 7624 kandikás or portions. In the

* Goldstücker's Literary Remains, i. p. 34.

Kánva recension it consists of seventeen kándas with a
hundred and four adhyáyas, four hundred and forty-six
bráhmanas, and five thousand eight hundred and sixty-
six kandikás. This Bráhmana furnishes us with the dogmatical, exegetical, mystical, and philosophical lucubra-
tions of early Brahman theologians and philosophers.
A partial examination of this book shows it to be
stamped with a character quite in harmony with that
of the Aitareya. And again these two works have
claims to be recognised as very ancient records of the
religious beliefs and rituals, and of the pristine institutions of Indian society. A story in the Satapatha illustrates the relations between the priestly and royal families in the early history of India; and gives us an
insights into the policy which actuated the Brahmans
to struggle from time to time for political influence. There
is also a legend of a deluge, in which Manu alone was
preserved for his sanctity and superior wisdom. According to this interesting legend he was not the creator of
man, but a representative of an earlier race of men.* The
legend of a flood, according to M. Burnouf, is not in
its origin Indian, but was most probably derived from a
Semitic source, whether Hebrew or Assyrian.† But Prof.
Weber from the legend of Manu in the Satapatha-Bráhmana, which he for the first time brought to light has
proved that the tradition was really current in India at a

---

* I. 8, I, I. See also Müller's Ancient Sanskrit Literature, pp. 425ff.;
Professor Williams' Indian Epic Poetry, p. 36; and Weber's Indische
Studien, I. 163 f.

† Bhágavata-Purána, iii. pp. 11, 41-47.

much earlier period than Burnouf thought ; and it was
not imported into that country from any of the Semitic
sources.* This Brâhmana may have been edited by Yâjnavalkya, but its principal portions, like those of the other
Brâhmanas, must have been accumulating for some period
before they were all aggregated and arranged into the sacred code of a new Charana. The Taittirîya-Brâhmana
may be regarded as a supplement to its Samhitâ ; but the
former does not differ from the latter so much in character
as in point of time.

There was originally only one text of each of the four
Vedas ; but each text passed through a large number of
Sâkhâs which gradually came into existence. A Sâkhâ
signifies an edition of a Veda. There was a class of
Sâkhâs, though of a confessedly later date, founded on
Sûtras, which derived their names from historical personages. However, there was originally a difference between a Sâkhâ and a Charana ; but these two words were
used generally as synonyms. Pânini speaks of Charanas
as comprising a number of followers.† If a Sâkhâ is used
in the sense of a Charana, this can only be accounted for
by the fact that in India the Sâkhâs did not exist not as
written books, but only in the tradition of the Charanas,
each member of a Charana representing and possessing a
copy of a book. A Sâkhâ as a portion of Sruti, cannot
properly include law books. But the adherents of certain
Sâkhâs might easily adopt a code of institutions which
would go by the name of their Charanas. In the Charana-

* Indische Studien, i. p. 100 ff.
† Pânini, iv. 2, 46.

vyûhs, a work ascribed to Saunaka, which treats of these
schools, there are enumerated five Sâkhâs of the Rig-veda;
and forty-two or in one recension forty-four out of eighty-
six are mentioned of the Yajur-veda. Twelve out of a
thousand are said to have once existed of the Sâman;
and of the Atharva-veda only nine.[*] But only a very
few of these editions have come down to us.

The Atharvasanrahasya, a modern treatise on the Atharva-veda, attributing the same number of Sâkhâs to the
Sâma-veda and the Atharva-veda, speaks of twenty-one of
the Rig-veda, and a hundred of the Yajur-veda. But of all
these Sâkhâs the Rig-veda is now extant only in one;
the Yajus in three, and we may say in four; the Sâman
perhaps in two; and the Atharvan in one. The only
recension in which the Samhitâ of the Rig-veda is
found, is that of the Sâkala school. The text of the Black
Yajus is extant in the recensions of the two schools, that
of A'pastamba, and that of the Kâthaka which belongs to
the Charakas; and the White Yajus exists in the recensions
of the Mâdhyandina and the Kânva schools. The Samhitâ of the Sâman is preserved in the two recensions: in
that of the Rântâyanîyas, and probably also that of the
Kauthumas. The text of the Atharvan is preserved only
in the Saunaka school. Each Sâkhâ claimed the possession of the only true and genuine Veda. The discrepancies between these Sâkhâs, however, consisted chiefly in
numerous variations of their arrangement of the sacred
scriptures and in their subsequent accretions or total
omissions of texts.

[*] Weber's Indische Studien, ziii. pp. ijxff.

Although Sâkhâ and Charana were sometimes used synonymously, yet Sâkhâ properly applies to the traditional text followed as in the phrase *sâkhâm adhîte*; and Charana an ideal succession of teachers and pupils. We should then understand by a Sâkhâ a traditional recension of any of the Vedas, handed down by different Charanas, or different schools or sects, which strictly adhered to their own traditional text and interpretation. The Brahmans themselves were fully aware of this difference between a Sâkhâ and a Charana. And it is highly probable that new Charanas on sacred texts peculiar to them, were established in case of gross or slight discrepancies in the text of the hymns, as well as divergences in the Brâhmanas, as a Sâkhâ always consisted of a Samhitâ and a Brâhmana.

A Parishad means an assembly or a settlement of Brahmans associated for the study of the Vedas;[*] and the Parishads might be the title of any book belonging to a Parishad. The law books lay down the number, age, and qualifications of the Brahmans who must have composed such an assembly to give decisive opinions on all subjects they would be referred to. The members of the same Charana might become fellows of different Parishads and *vice versâ.* The real ancestors of the Brahmans are eight in number; and eight gotras are again divided into forty-nine different gotras, and these constitute a still larger number of families. Gotras were confined to Brahmans as well as to Kshattriyas, and Vaisyas; and they depended on a community of blood corresponding to families. Cha-

* Vrihadâranyaka, vi. 2.

ranas existed among the priestly caste only ; and they
depended on the community of the sacred texts, and as
such they were merely ideal fellowships. All the Brahman families that keep and preserve sacred or sacrificial
fire claim a descent from the seven *Rishis.*[*] A Brahman
is bound by law to know to which of the forty-nine gotras
his own family belongs ; and in consecrating his own fire
he must invoke the ancestors who founded the gotra to
which he belongs. Such names as *gotra, varya, pakaha,*
and *gana* are all used in one and the same sense. And
these genealogies represent something real, and have an
historical value.

From the Brahmanas sprang those mystical and theosophical writings, the A'ranyakas and the Upanishads.
By the word A'ranyaka Pânini understands a forester.[†]
If the theosophical works called the A'ranyakas were extant during his time, he would have recognized them as a
portion of the sacred literature. The A'ranyakas are so
called, according to Sâyana, because they were read in the
forest, as if they were the text books of the anchorites,
whose devotions were purely spiritual.[‡] Of the A'ranyakas there are four extant, the Vrihad, the Taittirîya, the
Aitareya, and the Kaushîtaki. These, no doubt, belong
to a class of Sanskrit writings, the history of which has
not yet been properly investigated. Their style is full of
strange solecisms.[§] The A'ranyakas contain the quintes-

[*] Bhrigu, Angiras, Viswamitra, Vasishtha, Kasyapa, Atri and Agasti.
[†] वरणम् सूत्रे । iv. 2, 129.
[‡] Goldstucker's Pânini, p. 179 ; Weber's Indische Studien, v. p. 149.
[§] Cowell's Kaushitaki-Upanishad, p. vii.

sence of the Vedas and they only treat of the science of Bruhma. The A'ranyakas, as an enlargement upon the Bráhmanas, presuppose their existence. They are anterior to the Sútras, and likewise they are posterior to the Bráhmanas to which they form a kind of appendix.

The A'ranyakas discuss the obscure points of religion and philosophy, the nature of God, the creation of the world, and the relation of man to God and subjects of a like nature. The names of the authors are unknown to us, because their authorship was disclaimed on the ground that the productions would lose all their divine authority ; and also because those productions are mere compilations from other works. However they exhibit the very dawn of thought ; and the problems discussed in them are not in themselves modern ; but still modes of modern thought are not altogether wanting in them. And they abound also in passages which are . unequalled in any language, for grandeur, simplicity and boldness.

The original Upanishads, or the Mysteries of Theosophy, had their place in the A'ranyakas and the Bráhmanas. The most important of them are full of theosophy and philosophy. Max Müller has surmised that the word Upanishad "meant originally the act of sitting down near a teacher, of submissively listening to him," whence it came to mean "implicit faith, and at last truth or divine revelation."[*] It may even be supposed with some reason that these works derived their names from the mysteriousness of the doctrines contained in them ; and perhaps also from the mystical and obscure manner in which

* Müller's History of Ancient Sanskrit Literature, p. 319.

they propound them. It is very probable that in the time of Pánini, the works bearing the name of Upanishads were not in existence.* The Upanishads are mere compilations from other works; and the names of the authors of the principal ones are unknown. They are commonly in the form of dialogue; and in the main written in prose with occasional fragments of verse, but sometimes they are all in verse. The oldest among them may date as far back as the sixth century B. C. They are the Vrihadáranyaka, the Aitareya, the Chhándogya, the Taittiríya, the Isa, the Kena, the Prasna, the Katha, the Mundaka and the Mándúkya. The ordinary enumeration of them exceeds a hundred; but most of them are apocryphal. All the fifty-one were translated into Latin and published by Anquetil Duperron in 1801, under the title of "Oupnekhat" or "Theosophia Indica." His translations were mostly from a Persian version prepared by the orders of Dara Shukoh. The various systems of Hindu philosophy have their basis in the Upanishads, though quite antagonistic in their character. Most of the modern Upanishads are the works of Gaudapáda, Sankara, and other philosophers. Founders of new sects composed numerous other Upanishads of their own as the ancient ones did not suit their purpose.† The original Upanishads must ever occupy a prominent place in the sacred literature of the Indo-Aryans. The theological and philosophical

* Colebrooke's Pánini, p. 141.

† Ward's View of the History, Literature and Mythology of the Hindus, ii. p. 61.

speculations they contain are sublime productions of the human mind. They are the most ancient monuments of philosophical conceptions, and as such they are far more advanced both in the depth and loftiness of their ideas and opinions than any of the Greek schools prior to Socrates, except that of Elea. They contributed much towards the formation of the civil and domestic polity, and directed the whole tone of moral ordinances. They are considered with some show of reason as the highest authorities on which the various systems of philosophy are said to rest. The Vedânta philosopher seeks some warranty for his faith in the Veda ; and the Sânkhya, the Vaiseshika, the Nyâya and the Yoga philosophers profess to find in the Upanishads some authority for their opinions though there is no ground of harmony among them ; the chief object of the Upanishads being to unfold the darkest points of philosophy and religion, to discuss the creation of the world, to descant on the nature of God, and to elucidate the relation of man to God and the like. There is however not to be found any systematic uniformity in the Upanishads ; and the philosophy contained in them is as sublime as it is in some places puerile. Indeed, they have with some exceptions clearly distinguished the principle of spiritual existence ; and have successfully made the distinction between concrete existence and abstract being. But in fact the authors of them are merely poets rather than true philosophers, who throw out rhapsodies which are altogether unconnected and often contradictory, and seem to have no thought or even care of bringing into agreement to-day's feelings

with those of yesterday or of tomorrow." They shadow
forth the later Vedânta as the oracular denunciations
of Herakleitos shadow forth the complete developed
system of the Platonic philosophy. The reader of the
Upanishads finds no difficulty in recognising familiar ideas
in the rigid speculations of Plato as well as of Empedocles
or Pythagoras, in the Neo-platonism of the Alexandrian
school, as well as in the philosophy of the Gnostics. The
Upanishads contain mythological as well as theosophical
elements ; and they exhibit a freedom of thought which
was in fact the beginning of Hindû philosophy. And the
key-note of the old Upanishads is "Know thyself." The
Upanishads, from the beginning to the end, consist of texts
which propound that God is the one spirit, which is the
substance of the universe ; that the creation is nothing else
than a multiplication and development of Himself ; and
that the universe is to Him what the butter is to the milk.
They inculcate pantheism of one kind or another : but
their pantheism is, beyond doubt, of a very spiritual kind.
That theory of no two of them can be regarded precisely
the same. Some of them abound in speculations, much
after the fashion of development philosophers, on the physical primeval element of the universe ; and whatever is,
on the impulse of the moment accepted as a first principle,
is announced to be Brahma or God. The great teachers
of this parâ, or superior knowledge, were Kshattriyas, and
Brahmins are merely represented as becoming pupils of
the great Kshattriya kings. The Kshattriya mind first
carried on these bold speculations : and we can scarcely

avoid this conclusion when we add to this the remarkable
fact that the Gâyatri itself, the most sacred prayer of the
Brahmans, is a hymn by an author, not a Brahman but a
Kshattriya.* The Upanishads abound in descriptions not
merely of carnal observances; but also of obscenities still
worse and grosser than Jayadeva's battles of love.

The Brihadâranyaka constitutes the last five prapâthakas of the fourteenth book of the Satapatha-Brâhmana in
the Mâdhyandina-sâkhâ. The Upanishad properly so called
is divided into six chapters, and each chapter is again sub-
divided into different brâhmanas. It wears a purely speculative and legendary character; and deals with the doctrine
of the transmigration of souls. The Taittiriya-A'ranyaka
includes ten prapâthakas, of which the last four are styled
the Upanishad, and the first six are properly called the
A'ranyaka. It is throughout ritualistic, and represents the
latest period of Vaidik ideas. The sixth chapter of the
A'ranyaka gives in detail the whole of the funeral ceremonies required to be observed at burials. The Taittiriya-
Upanishad is a part of the Taittiriyâranyaka of the Black
Yajus. It is divided into three chapters, the Sikshâ-valli,
the Brahmânanda-valli, and the Bhrigu-valli. We trace in
it the germ of the Vedânta system. The Taittiriyâranyaka
is older than the Brihadâranyaka. It shows a strange medley
of post-Vaidik ideas and names. The Aitareyâranyaka
consists of five books and forms a work by itself; the
second and third books of which form the Bahvricha-Upa-
nishad. The first book is arranged in five chapters; the
second in seven; the third in two; the fourth in one;

* Virchand.

and the fifth in three. These chapters again are sub-divided
into a number of khandas. With reference to its subject,
the Aitareya may be divided into two parts, the first liturgical, and the second philosophical. This A'ranyaka is not
the work of the same individual; and the first three books
are said to be written under divine inspiration, and the rest
by human authors. The Aitareya is more speculative and
mystical than legendary or practical. There is another
A'ranyaka called the Kaushitaki-A'ranyaka, which is divided
into three books of which the third constitutes the Kaushitaki-Upanishad. This A'ranyaka treats more of ritual than
of speculation. The Kaushitaki-Upanishad consists of four
chapters; and there is no doubt that it is contemporaneous
with the Brihadaranyaka of the White Yajus.* There
are no A'ranyakas for the Sama-veda, nor for the Atharva-veda. The A'ranyakas derive their authority from
Sruti. Sáyana states that the Taittiríya-Upanishad comprises three parts, and they go by the names of Sánhitá,
Yájniki, and Váruni; of these the last is the most important, because it touches the knowledge of the Divine Self.
The Aitareya is included in the second A'ranyaka of the
Aitareya-Bráhmana. It contains three chapters. The
Taittiríya and Aitareya resemble each other in a great measure. The Svetásvatara is comparatively modern. In fact,
it does not belong to the series of the more ancient Upanishads. It was composed after the publication of the
Vedánta and Sánkhya; and is a compound of the Vedánta
pantheism and the Sánkhya duality. The Vájasaneyi-
Upanishad is very short. It is composed of only eighteen

* Weber's History of Indian Literature, p. 51.

sruti; and forms an index to the Vājasaneyi-Samhitā. The Talavakāra, or Kena-Upanishad, which is one of the shortest and the most philosophical treatises of this kind, puts in clearer language, perhaps, than any other Upanishad, the doctrine that the true knowledge of the Supreme Spirit consists in the consciousness which man acquires of his complete inability to understand him, since the human mind being capable only of comprehending finite objects, cannot have a knowledge of what is infinite. The Kena is included in both the Atharvan and the Sāman. The Katha has always been considered as one of the best Upanishads; and it must be admitted, that in point of elevation of thought, depth of expression, beauty of its imagery, and ingenious fervour, few stand equal to it. It consists of two adhyāyas, each of which contains three vallīs. The first part is quite independent. But the second is composed almost entirely of Vaidik quotations, which prove more in detail the doctrine enunciated in the first. It is on this account that both the parts are with some reason taken as two distinct Upanishads. There can be no doubt as to the second part being later than the first; and this is clear from several other, particularly linguistic, reasons. But Dr. Weber is of opinion that the Katha originally closed with the third vallī.* This Upanishad treats, first, of the highest object of man; second, the First Cause of the world and his attributes; third, the connexion of this Cause with the world. These questions are mooted in the different chapters in a manner which is quite peculiar to the Upanishads

* Weber's Indische Studien, ii pp. 197-300 ff

in general. The stand-point of the Katha is, however, on
the whole that of the scholastic doctrines of the Vedânta
philosophy. We cannot give the same credit to the philosophy as to the form of the Katha. There is scarcely any
link connecting the thoughts, so that they rather show
that it is plainly a compilation than the production of an
original and devout thinker. According to the Katha, the
knowledge of Brahma hangs upon a process of thinking.
i. e. it is derived from philosophy, and not from revelation.
The Prasna, one of the Upanishads of the Atharva-veda, is
divided into six chapters, each of which attempts to solve a
distinct question. From the first question we arrive at the
knowledge of the relation that exists between Prajâpati
and the creatures, the period of creation, and the manner
in which Prajâpati is to be worshipped. The description
is altogether mythological and symbolical, and does not
show any well-defined thought. The second shows his relation to the individual bodies. From the third question we
should understand that life, when produced from the soul, is
divided into the five vital airs, by whose regular actions
the functions of the body are sustained. The remaining
part of this question furnishes us with a specimen of the
anatomical and physiological knowledge of the author;
and a bold attempt to apply the functions observed in the
microcosm of the human body to the macrocosm of the
world. The fourth question is free from mythological
embellishments, and gives the substance of the doctrines
of the entire Upanishad.

The Mundaka-Upanishad contains three mandakas;
each of which is sub-divided into two khandas. There are

two sciences, according to the first mundaka, the *aparā* and the *parā*. The former is founded on the four Vedas and the six Vedāngas ; the latter refers to Brahma, that Being who is incomprehensible to the organs of action and intellect, and is without qualities. We find mention of the Vedānta and Yoga in this Upanishad. "It would almost be a contradiction in terms, to say that the Mundaka is a section of the Atharva-veda, which it condemns, along with the others, as inferior science. And if it must be referred to a post-Vaidik age, it would be difficult to affirm that it was composed before the age of Buddha."[*] The identity between the Katha, Prasna and Mundaka appears not merely in the mode of explanation, but also in the images and in entire passages. More particularly is this the case between the Mundaka and Katha than between the Mundaka and Prasna Upanishads. Which of these Upanishads was the original, or what relation they bear to other sources, can hardly be determined. This much, however, may be said, that the Prasna bears every mark of compilation. The Māndūkya has only twelve slokas. In these slokas the meaning of the mystical syllable *Om* is unravelled. This Upanishad is taken from various sources. From it, the contents having been stripped of their abstruse phraseology, we are to understand that Brahma comprehends all things, both objects of perception and those that are beyond the reach of perception. Brahma has four modes of existence, the waking state, the state of dreaming, the state of profound sleep, and a fourth state quite different from any of the former ; this state is indescribable, in which all manifestations cease, it is blissful and without duality. The Mâdûkya is one of the latest among the Upanishads which show the intimate spirit in its primitive nature, wholly uninfluenced by sectarian views. The order, in which the state of Brahma's existence is described, exhibits, on the whole, a very profound mode of thought. The Chhândogya-Upanishad consists of eight chapters. It is more modern than the Brihadâranyaka, which probably belongs to the eastern part of Hindustan.[*] In the Chhândogyopanishad a number of most curious modes of upâsanâ are prescribed. One of these devotions is so grossly obscene and filthy that we must refrain from translating or reproducing it here. The Bahvrichas placed Átman or the Self at the beginning of all things. The Taittiriyakas speak of Brahma as true, omniscient and infinite. Calling Brahma as neuter, they give proofs of their having been impressed with the idea of a Power. It was decidedly an era in the history of the human intellect when the apparent identity of the Self in the masculine, and Brahma in the neuter, was for the first time clearly established. The Chhandogas speak of a *Sat*, or a Being who has the tendency to be many. The A'tharvanikas speak of the Creator as *Akshara*; and it is very uncertain whether they used this word to mean Element or the Indestructible. The term used by the Vâjasaneyins is *Asyûlrita*, or the Undeveloped. The Upanishads are the principal parts of the Vedas. Of all the Vaidik works, they were the last composed.

The Mantras, the Brâhmanas, the A'ranyakas, and the

Upanishads are designated under the term of Sruti ; while
the term Smriti includes the Vedângas, the Sûtras, either
Srauta or Grihya, &c. Sruti means revelation, and Smriti
recollection. The Mantras are either metrical hymns or
prose forms of prayer, in which the praises of the gods are
celebrated, and their blessing is invoked. The Rik and
the Sâman consist of hymns of the former description.
The Brâhmanas arose out of the hymns, and so stand next
to them. They embrace liturgical regulations regarding
the ceremonial employment of the hymns, and the celebration of various rites and sacrifices ; and include also such
treatises as the A'ranyakas and the Upanishads. The A'ranyakas and Upanishads are theological treatises, which
bear the same character as do some of the older portions
of the Brâhmanas. They give very distinct indications of
spiritual aspirations, and also of ideas of a speculative and
mystical character such as we find in the hymns, and in
the earlier portions of the Brâhmanas ; but only with this
exception that in these treatises they have been further
matured as they developed in the minds of subsequent
generations of sages. The distinction between Sruti and
Smriti had been established by the Brahmans prior to
the rise of Buddhism, or prior to the time when the style
of the Sûtras gained admittance into Indian literature.
This difference, in fact, occurs in the Brâhmanas.* The
term Smriti is also met with in the Taittiríyâranyaka,†
though it is used there in the sense of Sruti. That Smriti
has no claim to an independent authority, but derives its

* Aitareya-Brâhmana, vii. 9
† Taittiríyâranyaka, I. 1. 2.

...nction from its relation to Sruti, is to be understood by its very name which means tradition. In the Sûtras the distinction is clearly made between Sruti and Smriti. We also find the same distinction in the Anupada-Sûtra.* And in the Nidâna-Sûtra ancient tradition is also mentioned under the name of Smriti.†

* Anupada-Sûtra, II. 4.
† Nidâna-Sûtra, II. 1.

CHAPTER V.

*The Peculiarities of the Sūtras—the Vedāngas—the
Origin and General Character of the Prātiśākhyas—
the Anukramanis—the Pariśishtas—the Origin
of Buddhism—the Knowledge of Writing
in ancient India.*

The Sūtra is the technical name given to aphoristic
rules, and also to those works which consist of such
rules. The Sūtras, upon the whole, rest, though not
entirely, upon the Brāhmanas. The importance of the
term, however, may be conceived from the fact, that the
groundworks of the whole ritual, grammatical, metrical,
and philosophical literature of India are indited in the
aphoristic style, which exhibits one of the peculiarities of Indian authorship. Though there is no clear
evidence as to the cause which gave birth to this pecu
liarity in Sanskrit composition; the method of in-
struction followed in ancient India renders it probable
that these Sūtras were so composed as to facilitate
the studies of pupils who had to learn simply by
heart. But it is also equally probable that this method of schooling itself gained ground owing to the

want of suitable materials for writing purposes, and in consequence of the expediency of economising those materials so far as could be possible. Thus great brevity and a rigid economy of words was practised. The Sûtra works are all brief, systematic, and enigmatical. Every doctrine thus propounded in them is so strained and twisted in every possible manner that it is almost reduced to mere algebraic symbols. The most obscure brevity is the principal object which guided the authors of the Sûtra works. "Even the bare simplicity of the design vanishes in the perplexity of the structure." Owing to curtness and elliptical obscurity these Sûtras are almost unintelligible. In fact, to acquire mastery over the Sûtra works is next to impossible, without the help of the key which is found in separate Sûtras called Paribhâshâ. Notwithstanding this key the student also must be in possession of the laws of the so-called Anuvritti and Nirvritti. They are certainly one of the most curious sorts of literary composition that the human mind has ever produced; and if altogether worthless in an artistic point of view, it is remarkable that the Indo-Aryans should have fabricated this most difficult form, and adopted it as the most convenient vehicle of expression of every branch of learning.

The elaborate and overstrained conciseness of the Sûtras renders them in a high degree obscure and ambiguous. Notwithstanding the key to their interpretations, there are to be found many seeming contradictions. The Sûtras bewilder even a scholar, and puzzle him at the very threshold in the obscure labyrinth of symbols and abbreviations. The Sûtra works contain the quintessence of all the knowledge which was then floating about in the Parishads, and which the Brahmans themselves had accumulated during many centuries of study and reflection. The cut and dry style of the Sûtra is so peculiar to India that it allows of no comparison with the style of composition of other countries in the early times when they were composed.

We have to search for the Vedânga doctrines in all their originality and authenticity in the Brâhmanas and the Sûtras ; and not in those barren tracts which are now known by the name of Vedângas. The Vedângas are not parts of the Vedas themselves, but supplementary to them ; and in the form in which we now possess them, are not wholly genuine ; and in fact, are of little importance. They are, however, auxiliary books for understanding the Vedas. All these works were written with an object of their being practical ; and they exhibit quite a novel phase in the literature of the ancient Indians. Their authors were not inspired, and the style which they employed to subserve their purpose, was business-like on the whole. Manu calls them Pravachanas,[*] a title which is usually applied to the Brâhmanas. We find the earliest mention of the six Vedângas in one of the Brâhmanas of the Sâman.[†] Yâska (Nir. i. 20) only quotes the Vedângas ; but he does not give the title of any of them. The number of the six Vedângas is given in the Charanavyûha, in Manu (iii. 185) and also in the Chhândogyopanishad. The Mundaka-panishad also gives us the entire number of the Vedângas.

---

* Manu, iii. 184.

† Shadvinsa-Brâhmana, iv. 7.

A clear statement as to the rational character of the Vedāngas is given in the Brihadāranyaka and in its commentary.

The first Vedānga is called Sikshā which, according to Sāyana, who lived in the 14th century A. D.,[*] comprises rules regarding letters, accents, quantity, organs, enumeration, delivery, and euphonic combinations. This little treatise is ascribed to Pānini; and it is possible that we may not find it to be an original Vedānga work. Pānini's Sikshā consists in one recension of thirty-five, and in another of fifty-nine verses. We have another tract on Sikshā, called the Mānduki-Sikshā, which is probably a later production of the Sūtra period; but it is of great importance as it bears the name of a certain Charana of the Rig-veda, the Māndukāyana. The rules on Sikshā had formerly a place in the seventh book of the Taittirī-yāranyaka; and Sāyana also takes the same view in his commentary on the Sāmhitā-Upanishad. In fact, this book is called the Sikshā chapter; and it is more than doubtful whether it was ever considered as such.[†] It is also supposed that these rules lost this place by the appearance of the Prātisākhya. But nothing is found in the Pushpa-Sūtra of Gobhila to prove this. The Sikshās are older than the Prātisākhya. Their doctrines, no doubt, were incorporated and highly developed in the latter.

The second is called Chhandas which treats of metre. But the Sākala Prātisākhya contains some chapters on

* Wilson's Rig-veda, I. p. xlvii ; Müller's Sanskrit Researches, p 137.
† Indian Antiquary, v. pp. 141 ff ; 169 ff.

metre, which are far more valuable than this utterly un-
important work known by the name of Chhandas. The
work of Pingalanaga on Chhandas, which is frequently
quoted under the title of Vedanga, is not of great antiquity ; and it becomes very doubtful whether it is an
original Vedanga work.[*] Some suppose Pingala was
the same as Patanjali, the author of the Mahabhashya.[†]
But the identity of Pingala and Patanjali is far from
being probable. It is not surprising that Pingala does
not confine himself exclusively to the metres of Sanskrit.
He also gives rules bearing on the metres of Prakrita ;
and even Katyayana-vararuchi, the author of the Vartti-
kas on Panini, the great Father of Sanskrit Grammar,
is said to have written a Prakrita grammar. It must be
admitted that the treatise of Pingala on Chhandas was
one of the last books that were included in the Sutra
period. Prof. Wilson supposes it to be scarcely regarded
as belonging to this period. But on no ground can we
exclude it from this period altogether. Pingala is quoted
as an authority on metre in the Paridishtas. We learn
from Shadgurusishya that Pingala was the younger brother,
or at least the descendant of Panini. And according to
some Pingala may be as old as the second century B. C.

The third is called Vyakarana. The Indo-Aryans
cultivated the science of grammar from the earliest times.
Eight different schools of grammar prevailed in India.
Panini's system undoubtedly superseded all other systems.
Of all these schools of grammar the Aindra was the

* Weber's History of Indian Literature, p. 66.
† Colebrooke's Essays, ii. p. 63.

object; and the treatises of that school are actually quoted by Pânini.* Pânini is the only representative of this Vedânga; and his grammar consists of eight adhyâyas or books, each adhyâya comprising four pâdas or chapters, and each pâda a number of sûtras or aphoristic rules. The latter amount on the whole to 3996 sûtras composed with the symbolic brevity of the most concise memoria technica; but three or four of them did not originally belong to the work. The sûtras are all made up of the driest technicalities; and their arrangement, on the whole, is based on the principle of tracing linguistic phenomena. In a general manner, Pânini's grammar may be called a natural history of the Sanskrit language. He records such phenomena of the language as are exceedingly interesting and valuable from a grammatical point of view. Words which he has treated of are also of historical and antiquarian interest. He also gives very useful information about the ancient geography of India. His grammar is built, no doubt, on the perfect phonetic system of which he was not altogether the inventor.† The source of Pânini's purely grammatical doctrines must be sought for elsewhere; and it is sufficiently evident that he quotes various grammarians who had preceded him. To fix the age in which Pânini lived, is a task we are incapable of performing; as many of the Indian authors shine, to use the words of a well-known Sanskrit scholar, like fixed stars in India's literary firmament, but no telescope can discover any appreciable dis-

---

* Burnell's Aindra Grammarians, p. 2.

† Weber's History of Indian Literature, p. 216.

meter. However it must be of some interest to know whether that Patriarch of Sanskrit Philology is likely to have lived before or after the death of Buddha. According to the views expressed by Prof. Goldstücker it is probable that Pânini lived before Buddha, the founder of the Buddhist religion, whose death took place about 543 B. C. ; but that a more definite date of the great Grammarian can hardly be obtained in the present condition of Sanskrit philology. Müller holds Pânini to be anterior to Yâska, but Yâska is noticed by Pânini himself ;[*] and there can be no doubt that Pânini was posterior to Yâska. Pânini was a native of Salâtura, situated in the Ghandhâra country north-west of Attock on the Indus. Whence he is also called Sâlâturiya. His mother was called Dâkshi. He was a descendant of Pânin, and grandson of Devala. He belonged, therefore, to the north-western or western school.

The Mahâbhâshya by Patanjali is not a full commentary of Pânini, but with some exceptions, only a commentary on the Vârttikas or critical remarks of Kâtyâyana on Pânini ; and so it is rather a controversial manual. From circumstantial evidence Prof. Goldstücker has proved that Patanjali wrote his Mahâbhâshya between 140 and 120 B. C.[†] Kâtyâyana, the critic of the great Grammarian was most likely the same with the Kâtyâyana who wrote the grammatical treatise called the Prâtisâkhya of the White Yajus. Goldstücker has further shown that

* Pânini, ii. 4. 63. वरुणंतुदति वा । See also Lassen's Indian Antiquities, i. pp. 864-866, ii. p. 476

† Pânini : His Place in Sanskrit Literature, p. 235f.

he could not have been the contemporary of Pâini as is generally supposed. He has also proved that this Kâtyâyana was the contemporary of Patanjali ; and probably being the teacher of the latter, he must have lived in the middle of the second century before Christ.[*] Kâtyâyana completed and corrected Pâini's grammar ; and his Vârttikas show a more wide and profound knowledge of Sanskrit than the work of Pâini himself. We obtain some information about Kâtyâyana from the Kathâsaritsâgara, the encyclopædia of legends, by Somadeva Bhatta of Kashmir. But after all we are to reject it as an episode in the story of a ghost. Somadeva composed it for the entertainment of the grand-mother of Srî Harshadeva, king of Kashmir, who ascended the throne of that country in 1059 and reigned, according to Abo 'l fazel, only 13 years ; and consequently it must have been written between 1059 and 1071, or a few years earlier. The Kathâsaritsâgara is supposed by many to be the sheet-anchor of Indian chronology.

There are two other works on grammatical subjects the Unâdi-Sûtras and the Phit-Sûtras of Sântanâchârya. As to when Sântana's Phit-Sûtras were composed we are perfectly in the dark. Pâini does not presuppose a knowledge of them ; and the grammatical terms employed by Sântana are quite different from those adopted by Pâini. Although those Sûtras treat simply of accents, and accents such as are used in the Vaidik language ; the subject of Sântana's work does not warrant us to suppose that he was

* Weber's Indische Studien, xiii p. 397, &c.

anterior to Pâṇini. "The Uṇâdi-Sûtras are rules for deriving, from the acknowledged verbal roots of the Sanskrit, a number of appellative nouns, by means of a species of suffixes, which, though nearly allied to the so-called *krits*, are not commonly used for the purposes of derivation." . . . . "A peculiarity of all words derived by an uṇâdi is, that, whether they be substantives or adjectives, they do not express a general or indefinite agent, but receive an individual signification, not necessarily resulting from the combination of the suffix with a verbal root."[*] The Uṇâdi-Sûtras we now possess, are not in their original form. It was not the object of the author to give a complete list of all the uṇâdi words, but merely to collect the most important of them. In fact, these were originally intended for the Veda only, and subsequently enlarged by the addition of rules on the formation of non-Vaidik words. It is not known by whom the Uṇâdi-Sûtras were first collected. Pâṇini frequently refers in his Sûtras to a list of affixes or uṇâdis, but not to the Uṇâdi-Sûtras.[†] It is, therefore, probable that those affixes must have existed before his time.[‡] By some the Uṇâdi-Sûtras are ascribed to Śâkaṭâyana, an ancient grammarian anterior to Yâska, and a Sûdra and follower of Buddha. But a very interesting passage in Virali's Bṛhapaṁâlâ distinctly ascribes the authorship of the Uṇâdi-Sûtras to Vararuchi who is no other than Kâtyâyana.[¶]

---

[*] Aufrecht's Uṇâdi-Sûtras, p. ⋆.
[†] Pâṇini, ul. 3, 1 ; lul. 4. 75
[‡] Müller's History of Ancient Sanskrit Literature, p 151.
[¶] Ibid. p. 240.

The fourth Vedānga is the Nirukta of Yāska, the oldest
glossator on the Veda. The Nirukta is a sort of commentary on the Nighantus ; and it is found frequently to refer
to the Brāhmanas, and bring forward various legends such
as those about Devāpi (xi. 10) and Visvāmitra (ii. 24). The
Nirukta is older than Pānini. Yāska also furnishes us with
the names of no less than seventeen interpreters who had
preceded him ;[*] but their explanations of the Veda generally
conflict with one another. The Nighantus comprise a
vocabulary of synonymous, obsolete, and obscure Vaidik
forms. The Nighantus and Nirukta are closely connected ; the former is older than the latter. Yāska ascribes the Nighantus to an ancient tradition. If the
Nirukta belongs to Yāska, the Nighantus also could not
have been written by him. However to the Nirukta we are
inclined to attribute a very high antiquity ; it belongs to
the oldest part of Sanskrit literature excepting the Vaidik
writings, and to an already far advanced period of grammar and interpretation.

Yāska prefixed the Nighantus to his own work,
the Nirukta, in which he throws light on the obscure passages of the Vedas. The Nirukta consists of three parts.
The first part or the Naighantuka comprises a collection of synonymous words, the second or Naigama a collection of words peculiar to the Vedas, and the third or
Daivata words relating to deities and sacrifices. In this
Vedānga we find the first fundamental notions of grammar.
It is obvious that when this work of Yāska was composed,

* Roth's Illustrations, pp. 2ff . see also Weber's History of Indian
Literature, p. 35.

and even at a much earlier period, the sense of most of
the Vaidik words had become completely obscure. This
clearly appears from the fact of such works as the Nighantus and Nirukta being written at all. The Nirukta
together with the Prâtiśâkhyas and the grammar of Pânini
supplies the most important information on the growth of
grammatical science in India. Yâska is wholly unacquainted
with such algebraical symbols as are contained in Pânini.
The introduction to the Nirukta, which supplies us with a
full sketch of a grammatical and exegetical system, gives
the views of Yâska and his predecessors; and it is in
this manner we are able to establish a complete comparison
of these older grammarians with Pânini.

The fifth is the Kalpa or the Ceremonial. The Brâhmanas are the sources of the Vaidik ritual, which became
completely developed and systematised in the ritual works
called the Kalpa-Sûtras. The composition of the Kalpa-
Sûtras is in some respects an important event in the
Vaidik history. Though they do not claim to be Smritis,
yet they are enumerated amongst the Smâdhyâyas. The
Kalpa-Sûtras must have been drawn up for the easy reference of the priests, who would otherwise have to grope
in the dark through the liturgical Samhitâs and Brâhmanas for the disjecta membra of the sacrificial and other
rites. Thus we possess Kalpa-Sûtras connected with the
Rig-veda by Âśvalâyana, Sânkhâyana and Saunaka;
with the Sâma-veda by Masaka, Lâtyâyana, Gobhila,
Drâhyâyana, and a Sûtra called Anupada-Sûtra; with
the Black Yajur-veda by Âpastamba, Baudhâyana, Satyâ-
shâdha-Hiranyakesin, Mânava, Bhâradvâja, etc.; with the

White Yajur-veda by Kátyáyana; and with the Atharva-veda by Kusika. There is another Kalpa work belonging to the Atharva-veda, which is called the Vaitána-Sútra; and which cannot claim a very remote antiquity. The Vaitá-na-Sútra presupposes the existence of the Kausika-Sútra. Kátyáyana also takes notice of this Sútra work. It bears the same relation to the Gopatha-Bráhmaṇa as does the Aśva-láyana Srauta-Sútra to the Aitareya-Bráhmaṇa.* Though it is a Srauta-Sútra of the Atharvas it was composed under the influence of the Yajus. It does not contain at all magical hymns and conjurations; but it contains much interesting matter which we do not find in other ritual works.† The Kalpa-Sútras are divided into three classes, such as Srauta, Grihya, and Sámayáchárika: the first prescribe the especial Vaidik ceremonials, such as those which are to be celebrated on the days of new and full moon. The rites according to the Srauta-Sútras can be performed by rich people and no others; and have therefore been made obligatory only under certain restrictions. The second enjoins the domestic rites to be performed at various stages of life from birth to death. The Grihya-Sútras give general rules which are to be observed at marriages, at the birth of a child, on the day of naming the child, at the tonsure and investiture of a boy, and at the time of and after the death of a person. Indeed, the Grihya-Sútras contain all the rules bearing on those principal and purificatory ceremonies which are included under the

* Haug's Aitareya-Bráhmaṇa I. p. 8; see also Weber's History of Indian Literature, p. 57.

† Garbe's Vaitána-Sútra, pp. v.-xii; see also Weber's Indische Studien, 2. p. 176; and Roth's Atharva-veda in Kashmir, p. 2.

general name of *samskáras*° or certain sacramental rites.
The rites and ceremonies according to the Grihya are
called Pákayajna or sacrifices with food. A Pákayajna
consists in a piece of wood being placed in the fire in a
hearth, oblations made to the gods, and gifts bestowed on
the Brahmans. The third regulates the daily observances
of the twice born. The rules of the Sámayáchárika-Sútras
are based rather on secular than sacred authority. They
describe the duties of a student as a Brahmachárin or
catechumen in the house of his preceptor. They regulate
the proper diet of a Brahman. They prescribe what food
is allowable and what not ; what days should be allotted
for fasting ; and what penances ought to be performed for
not observing duty. They decide, in a great measure,
the duties and rights of kings and magistrates, the civil
rights of the people at large, and even rules of social
politeness. Of the Grihya-Sútras of the Ṛig-veda, we
have those by Sánkháyana and A'svaláyana ; a Grihya-
Sútra of the Sáma-veda is that of Gobhila ; of the Black
Yajur-veda we possess the Baudháyana ; and of the White
Yajur-veda, the Páraskara Grihya-Sútras. The Dráhyáyaṇa
belongs to the school of the Ráṇáyaníyas.   It differs but
slightly from the Látyáyana, and treats, on the whole, of
the same identical matter. The Látyáyana belongs to the
school of the Kauthumas. The first seven prapáthakas of
the Látyáyana-Sútras contain the injunctions applicable
to all the Soma sacrifices ; the 8th and part of the 9th prapáthaka treat of the *ekáhas* ; the remainder of the 9th of
the *ahínas* ; and the 10th of the *sattras* or sessions.

° Cf. Wilson's Dictionary, s. v.

The Kalpa-Sûtras mark a new period in the literary
and religious history of India; and they contributed,
no doubt, to the total extinction of the numerous Brâhmanas. From a comparison of the Brâhmanas with the
Kalpa books it appears that the difference between them
is of great importance. They are found to treat in the
most elaborate manner of the entire system of divine
worship, each in a quite different way. The Kalpa
books establish the whole course of the rites of worship.
They direct which of the priests have to take part
at each of the stages of the sacred rites, what hymns
are to be recited, and further define the time and
place for the celebration of those rites. But the object
of a Brâhmana is very different from the Kalpa works;
its subject being the "brahma," the sacred element in
the rite; from which we are to draw the most valuable
information regarding the early conceptions on divine
matters.* At any rate, the introduction of a Kal-
pa-Sûtra was the introduction of a new book of
liturgy. The Srauta and Grihya-Sûtras are of much
greater value than the Sâmayâchârika. The Grihya
and Sâmayâchârika-Sûtras have generally been con-
founded; but the Brâhmana draw a line of demar-
cation between the two, the Grihya-ceremonies being
performed by the married house-holder with no other
purpose than for the benefit of his family. The Srauta-
Sûtras mean the whole body of the Sûtras, the source of
which can be traced to the Sruti or the literature of
revelation, the Mantras and Brâhmanas; while the Smârta-

* Roth's Introduction to the Nirukta, p. xxiv, ff.

Sûtras can have claim to so such source. The main difference between the two lies not in their matter ; but in the age and style of composition. The Srauta-Sûtras treat of the grand and public religious ceremonies, rites and sacrifices (Haviryajnas and Somayajnas). Both the Grihya and Sâmayâchârika-Sûtras are included under the common title of Smârta-Sûtras in opposition to the Srauta-Sûtras. The former derived their authority from the Smriti, and the latter from the Sruti. The Sâmayâchârika-Sûtras are also called Dharma-Sûtras, and they seem to have been the source of the Dharma-sâtras.[*] The Kalpa-Sûtras are a complete system of ritualism, and give the whole method of the sacred ceremonial with great precision. It is not yet proved that the Kalpa-Sûtras are a part of the Vedas ; and in fact it is impossible to do. They were composed contemporaneously with Pânini. We are here to observe once for all that there are ten Sûtras of the Sâma-Veda ; and these Sâma-Sûtras do not all treat of the Kalpa or the Ceremonial. Some of them are more than mere lists, and their style approaches that of the Sûtras. The ritual work called the Mânava-Kalpa-Sûtras, which is connected with the Taittiriya-Samhitâ, sets forth or sanctions, more than the other Kalpa-Sûtras, the dogmas and conclusions of the Mimânsâ philosophers. This Kalpa-work is later than the Sûtras of Baudhâyana and older than those of A'pastamba.[†] During the time of the composition of these Sûtra works, the whole system of social organisation was developed, and

---

[*] Morley's Digest of Indian Cases, p. xxvi.
[†] Goldstücker's Pânini, p 12.

the distinction of caste was fully established. On examining the Sûtra works and especially the Grihya-Sûtras we find that women had no right to the use of the Vedas. Yet, we learn from the same source that the husband in conjunction with his wife performed sacrifices and other rites. Women were allowed to repeat mantras at the time of sacrifices; and they were never scrupulously or entirely denied the knowledge of God.

The sixth and last of the Vedângas is Jyotisha. Works of astronomy were very scanty; and the only copy we now possess of it is comparatively modern, and its literature is also very meagre. The Jyotisha is a short tract embracing thirty-six verses, which are composed in a comparatively modern style. Its main object is to offer only such information about the heavenly bodies as were useful in fixing the days and hours of the Vaidik sacrifices and not to teach astronomy as a science.

The Prátiśákhyas were designated Charanas, because they were the property of the readers of certain Sâkhâs. They are really a sub-division of the Párshads books. The Párshada is another title often applied to the Prátiśákhyas. The existing representatives of the Prátiśákhyas, in all probability, were composed subsequent to the age of Pâņini;* and most of their rules are intended to supply the deficiencies in the Sûtras of that grammarian. The Prátiśákhyas are nothing more than "theological and mystical dreams"; but they are not altogether destitute

* Goldstücker's Pâņini, p. 183 ff.; Müller's Rig-veda Prátiśákhya, Introduction; Weber's Indische Studien, xiii p. 3 ff., and his History of Indian Literature, p. 34.

of exegetical or critical value. There is no doubt that
they were written for practical purposes, and their
style is free from cumbrous ornaments and unnecessary
subtleties. Their object is to teach rather than to edify.
A great number of authors are referred to in the
Prátisákhyas, and opinions with general precepts are
found in them. Though we do not possess the works of
the earlier authors, yet we may fairly assume that their
favourite doctrines were treasured up originally in the
shape of Prátisákhyas. These writings contain rules on
accent, Sandhi, or the permutation of sounds, the length-
thening of the vowels in the Vedas, &c. The Kuladhar-
mas could not be called Prátisákhyas; but they might
claim the title of Charana or Párshada.

There are Prátisákhyas belonging to the Rig-veda, the
Yajur-veda, and the Atharva-veda. The oldest among
them is the Rig-veda-Prátisákhya. But when the Taittiriya-
Prátisákhya or the Kátyáyana-Prátisákhya originated we
cannot approximately say. The rules of the Prátisákhyas
were not merely a guide in the instructions of pupils who
had to learn the texts of the Vedas by heart; but they
were no doubt intended also for written literature. According to the representation of the Prátisákhyas there
are three modes of writing the Vedas, viz., the Samhitá-
pátha, the Pada-pátha, and the Krama-pátha. The
Samhitá-pátha means the mode of writing according to
the rules of permutation; the Pada-pátha separates single
words. And the Krama-pátha is two-fold, viz., the
Varna-krama and the Pada-krama. The Varna-krama always doubles the first consonant of a group of consonants;

and the Pada-krama takes two words of the sentence
together, and always reiterates the second of them with
a following one. Of all the Prátisákhyas of the numerous
Vaidik Samhitás, the Prátisákhya belonging to the Sákala-
sákhá is by far the most complete.

There is another class of Sútra works called the Anukramanis. The Anukramani to the Rig-veda is perfect in
every respect. It is called the Sarvánukramani which gives
the first word of each hymn, the number of the verses, the
names and families of the authors, the names of the deities to
whom hymns are addressed, and the metre of every verse.
Before the Sarvánukramani was composed there existed separate indexes for each of the subjects, which were ascribed
to Saunaka. The Sarvánukramani is said to have been
composed by Kátyáyana. The Brihaddevatá of Saunaka
being very voluminous, is not reckoned among the Anukramanis. It is composed in epic metre and contains an enumeration of the gods invoked in the hymns of the Rig-
veda ; and further supplies much valuable mythological
information about the character of the deities of the Vedas.
It is not unreasonable to suppose, judging from the
general tenor and style of the Brihaddevatá, that it was
recast by a later writer. The Brihaddevatá belongs to a
much later period than most of the Sútras ; and it is, in
fact, based upon the work of Yáska.[*] Dr. Kuhn infers
from a passage in Shadguruśishya's commentary that not
Saunaka but A'svaláyana was the author of the Brihaddevatá. This inference, however, is not supported by suffi-

cient evidence. Saunaka writes in mixed slokas and breaks in many cases the laws of metre. Kâtyâyana writes in prose much after the fashion of the later Sûtras. The relation between Saunaka and Kâtyâyana was very intimate; and both of them belonged to the same Sâkhâ. But it is probable that Saunaka was anterior to Kâtyâyana. The time of Shadgurusishya is not known. Probably his work was composed towards the close of the twelfth century.[*] There are three Anukramanis for the Yajur-veda, two for the Sâma-veda, and one for the Atharva-veda.[†]

The Rig-veda hymns are arranged according to two methods; the one having regard to the material bulk, and the other according to the authorship of the hymns. According to the former the whole Samhitâ consists of 8 ashtakas or eighths; these again are divided into 64 adhyâyas or lectures; these into 2006 vargas or sections; and the vargas into richas or verses, the actual number of which is 10,417; and some say that they amounted to 10,616 or 10,622. According to the other method, the Samhitâ is divided into 10 mandalas or circles; the mandalas into 85 anuvâkas or lessons, these into 1017 sûktas or hymns, besides eleven spurious ones, called Vâlakhilyas, and these again containing 10,580 and a half richas. The number of padas or words in this Samhitâ is stated as being 153,826, and that of the syllables is 432,000. The Nirukta mentions the Rig-veda in several places and always with the designation of Dasatayya or the ten parts. And the same mode of designation is also found in the

[*] Weber's Indische Studien, viii. p. 160, a.
[†] Müller's History of Ancient Sanskrit Literature, p. 215 ff.

Prátisákhya-Sútras. Another instance of the systematic
arrangement of the mandalas is contained in the A'pri-
hymns ; and there are only ten A'pri-Súktas attached to
the Ŕig-veda. These Súktas consist properly of eleven
verses, each of which is addressed to a separate deity ; and
they were evidently composed for sacrificial purposes.
They, however, throw light on the social condition of the
Indo-Aryans. The chief object of the A'pri hymns
is not easy to explain. It is probable that the A'pri
hymns were songs of reconciliation. Saunaka has given
different names of metres in an Anukramani. There
are three Anukramanis to the Yajus. The Sáman has
two different Anukramanis. For the Atharvan, there
is only one Anukramani which is called the Brihatsarvánu-
kramani. The style of composition and the object of the
different Anukramanis distinctly prove that they were
framed at the close of the Vaidik age.[*]

There is a class of works commonly designated Parisishtas. They have Vaidik rituals and sacrifices for their
subject-matter. It is said that most of the Parisishtas
are the productions of Saunaka, &c. The Parisishtas
represent a distinct period of Indian literature, and they
are evidently later than the Sútras. Such literary works
as the Parisishtas must be considered as the last outskirts
of Vaidik literature. But still they are Vaidik in character.
The Parisishtas, on the whole, are indited in simple and
felicitous diction. They were originally eighteen in number, but that number has now considerably exceeded.
The Charanavyúha, though itself a Parisishta, supports

this statement. There are a number of Parisishtas for each of the Vedas. For the Rig-veda there are only three, for the Sama-veda the number is only six; and according to the Charanavyuha there exist eighteen Parisishtas for the Yajur-veda. But Prof. Weber fixes their number at seventy-four. The object of the Parisishtas is to supply the deficiencies in the Sûtras. They treat every thing in a popular and superficial manner. None of them were written probably before the middle of the third century, B. C. Though the Parisishtas are not held in the same estimation as other Vaidik works, yet they contain very interesting 'indications of the progress and decay of Hindû thought.

In former times the Vedas were the only source of knowledge and truth to the Hindûs. No one then ventured to carry on any controversy, or hold or spread any doctrine unwarranted by them, it being universally assumed that all doctrines must be based on, and all controversies must end in, what was taught by the Vedas. It was considered the height of atheism to speak one word against them. Thus it was that the supreme and unerring authority of the Vedas having been established, all theological controversy was at once nipped in the bud. On the other hand, the study of the Vedas became gradually extinct ; the understanding and explaining of their meanings became a hard task ; the aims and objects of the yajnas, enjoined in them, were lost ; and all religious works came to be encrusted with external ceremonies. In every country where religion becomes so dead and lifeless, religious changes begin to creep in. So did it

fare with the Indian society. First of all Sâkya, the
founder of Buddhism, a man of uncommon wisdom and
courage, opposed the Vedas, exposed the futility and un-
reasonableness of such of their doctrines as the killing of
animals, and proved them to be of human origin. Men
were surprised at the first starting of these novel theories
of Sâkya. They had long ago relinquished the use of reason under the despotic government of the Vedas ; but
now again they entered the field of religious investigation, laid open by Sâkya with renewed earnestness.
But Sâkya was not the first who opposed the selfish priesthood. Several centuries before him, Visvâmitra of the
royal caste refused to submit to the hierarchical preten-
sions of the Brahmans, and succeeded in obtaining the
privileges for which he determinately fought. King
Janaka of Videha followed him in the same track.
The spread of Buddhism was simply owing to the fact
that it aimed at social reform, and more so to its pure
and simple morality rather than to the strength of its
doctrinal points.

The doctrines of such a man as Sâkya naturally began
to spread with the rapidity of fire borne by driving winds,
and India became a spacious field for the waging of
religious wars. Thus, within a short period, the Buddhists
waxed very strong in this country ; in the reign of Asoka,
king of Magadha, the greater portion of it was converted
to the religion of Sâkya. The Brahmans again roused
themselves and determined upon putting down the victorious heretics. With this view they went into every part
of the country, stirred up the dormant spirit of the Hindû

kings, and fell to religious debates with the Buddhists. In this momentous religious warfare Sankara A'chârya, who flourished in the 8th or 9th century,[*] played a most conspicuous and glorious part. He as a hermit visited alone every part of India, defeated the Buddhists, one and all, with the sharpedged acuteness of his intellect, his extraordinary wisdom and knowledge of the Vedas, and finally carried the palm of universal conquest. Thus, being borne down in debate by the Brahmans, and persecuted by kings, the Buddhists left India to spread their religion in other countries.[†] But though the Buddhists were themselves expelled from the country, their doctrines did not all follow them out of it ; on the contrary, these doctrines began, day by day, to strike deep root. And the doctrines of Sâkya were a refuge even for Brahmans, who were unable to master the extreme difficulties of their own complicated systems.[‡] The transcendental doctrine of Nirvâna, or total annihilation, which Sâkya had proclaimed, was carefully picked up and and nursed by the Hindú philosophers. Buddhism if examined by its own canonical works, cannot be freed from the charge of Nihilism. Sâkya himself not a Nihilist, was apparently an atheist. He does not gainsay either the existence of gods or that of God ; but he denounces the former, and seems to be ignorant of the latter. If Nirvâna was not complete annihilation, it at any rate according to him, was absorption in the Divine essence. It was a relapse

* Colebrooke's Essays, I. p. 332.
† Troyer's Radjatarangini, ii. p. 300.
‡ Burnouf's History of Indian Buddhism, p. 196.

into that Being which is nothing but itself. The original meaning of Nirvâna we can best know from the etymology of this technical term. Even a tyro in Sanskrit knows that Nirvâna means 'blowing out' and not absorption. The human soul when it reaches the acme of its full perfection, is blown out,[*] to use the phraseology of the Buddhists, like a lamp; it is not however absorbed, as the Brahmans say, like a drop in the ocean. We can not at all events accept the term Nirvâna in the sense of an apotheosis of the human soul as it is taught in the Vedânta philosophy. It admits of question whether the term Nirvâna was coined by Sâkya. Not merely different schools, but one and the same among the Buddhists appears to propound different theories as to the orthodox lexicography of this term.

The religion of the Vedas is an absurd system; Buddhism is equally absurd, but more philosophic. Buddhism was a revolt against the oppressive domination of the Brahmanic hierarchy. The devotion of the Buddhist ascetic was more disinterested. The Brahman idea of perfection was of an egotistical character. The meek spirit of Buddhism contrasts strongly with the haughtiness and arrogance of Brahmanism. We do not mean, however, to write the history of Buddhism; and we must, therefore, be satisfied with having given above a short sketch of a great revolution which occurred even in the Vaidik period.

There is one more circumstance in connexion with the subject to which we wish to allude, before we close,

[*] Amara-kosha, s. v.

and it has reference to the introduction of writing in ancient India. The greater portion of the vast ancient literature of India existed in oral tradition only, and was never reduced to writing. No man of any intelligence can easily imagine a civilized people unacquainted with the art of writing. If we are to understand that Hindú civilization could exist without a knowledge of writing, then it is needless to make reference to the arts, sciences, coins and measures, mentioned by Pánini in his Sútras. From a certain rule of his (iv. 1, 49) we are convinced of the fact that he knew that writing was practised in countries beyond India. In that rule he teaches the formation of the word Yavanání. Kátyáyana and Patanjali define Yavanání as meaning 'the writing of the Yavanas.' The word Yavana occurs in Homer as Iaones which is no doubt connected with the Hebrew Yavan. There can be no doubt that the Macedonian or Bactrian Greeks were the people most usually intended by the term. In later times it denoted especially the Arabs; but in earlier times it was exclusively applied to the Greeks as is evident from a passage quoted in the commentary of Pánini's grammar, 'yavanáí sayáná bhunjate,' which alludes, no doubt, to Greek customs. Weber[*] and not Müller[†] appears to give the meaning of the word Yavanání as the writing of the Greeks alone; but the latter would have us understand by it only a variety of the Semitic alphabet. M. Reinaud has given cogent reasons that Yavanání means the writing of the Greeks. Benfey also understands by it 'Greek

[*] Indische Studien, i. p. 144 ; ibid. iv. p. 92.
[†] History of Ancient Sanskrit Literature, p. 521.

writing.' *Yavanani* was generally used to signify *lipi* or writing; and probably refers to the alphabet of the Greeks.

Müller says that in the grammar of Pánini there is not a single word which shows that the Hindús knew the art of writing even when that learned work was composed. This assertion is a most novel and startling one, in as much as it is hard to conceive that a grammar, like that of Pánini, could be elaborated as it is now, without the advantage of written letters and signs in the days of the author. Kátyáyana and Patanjali not merely presuppose a knowledge of writing in Pánini, but also affirm that the use he made of writing was one of the chief means which enabled him in building up the technical structure of his work. Any person that has ever looked into Pánini must know that written accents were indispensable for his terminology. Pánini uses accents as written signs. The *swarita* is the mark of an *adhikára* or heading rule,* which showed a perpendicular line over the syllable; and the *anudátta* a horizontal line under it. But the syllable which is without any such marks is *udátta*. Pánini not unfrequently refers in his Sútras to the grammarians who had preceded him; which circumstance strengthens the argument in favor of the fact that writing was known even before Pánini's time. Pánini teaches the formation of the word *lipikara* (iii. 2, 21); which can be adduced in all fairness, to prove that the greatest Grammarian of India was acquainted with the art of writing. The use of the term Patala, meaning a

* Pánini. L 3, 11 : अधिकारः ।

division of Sanskrit works, is a further proof that writing was known in ancient India.

The authors of the Sûtra works are found to apply the term patala to the short chapters of their works. It is, however, wholly absurd to suppose that chapters can be so called in a traditional work. It is only possible in a written one. Patala is almost synonymous with *liber* and *biblos*. "There is no word, says Müller, 'for book, paper, ink, writing, &c., in any Sanskrit work of genuine antiquity."[*] This assertion of Müller clearly shows that he has overlooked some words which might have, on the contrary, removed all his doubts. He should have known that the object of the Vaidik hymns is not to tell us that the Indo-Aryans had reed and ink. It is most difficult to suppose that the human mind could ever be capable of composing in prose, volume after volume, on rituals, long series of commentaries, and elaborate works on theology, grammar, and lexicography without the help of written letters. According to Wolf, prose composition is an evident and safe proof of a written literature as poetry without being committed to paper, could be easily composed and transmitted from one generation to another traditionally; but to compose any thing in prose is impossible without the help of writing; and still more impossible to transmit it from one generation to another and preserve it in its entirety traditionally.[†] There are undoubtedly records of astronomical observations which could not have been taken without the knowledge of numerical figures. We cannot

* History of Ancient Sanskrit Literature. p. 512.
† Wolf's Prolegomena, Introduction.

help believing by the exact definition of words, which
appear in Pânini, such as varṇa, kâra, kânda, pattra,
sûtra, adhyâya, grantha, &c., that the use of written letters
was not unknown in ancient India. The meaning of
the word grantha is to string together, signifying the
old method of stringing together a number of palm
leaves, which constituted the chief material of books, just
as in German a volume is called *Band* from its being
'bound'. Prof. Weber holds that Pânini was perfectly acquainted with the art of writing; and the word grantha,
which is frequently used by Pânini, alludes, according to its
etymology, indisputably to written texts.[*] It answers
etymologically to the Latin *textus*, as opposed to a traditional work. But Böhtlingk and Roth say, on the contrary, that the word grantha refers merely to the composition.
Indeed, it may mean a literary composition. *Varṇa*
applies only to a written sign; and *kâra* to an uttered
sound, and also to a written sign. *Akshara* means syllable;
and may sometimes therefore coincide in value with *kâra*
and *varṇa*. *Akshara* signifying 'syllable' first occurs in
the Saṃhitâ of the Yajus. The word is also twice met
with in the Rik; and there it signifies the measuring of
speech (i. 164, 24 (47), and ix. 12, 8), and therefore may
be used in the sense of 'syllable.' The Commentaries of
Kâtyâyana, Patanjali and Kaiyyata prove that Pânini's
manner of defining an *adhikâra* (l. 3, 11), or heading
rule, would have been impossible without writing. Here
we will draw the attention of the reader to two words,
ûrdhva and ûdaya. The former is used adverbially in the

* Indische Studien. iv. p. 89.

sense of *after.*[*] It seems to us that the metaphorical sense
of the word was first applied to passages in written books.
The word ádaya is synonymous with árdhva. Pánini
speaks of repha. Even Kátyáyana arguing from its root,
concludes that it is nothing else than ra itself; and the
letter repha is found to be used in the Prátisákhyas. The
use of repha is also a proof that Pánini was not ignorant
of writing. Grantha occurs four times in the text of
Pánini; and it is evident, beyond doubt, that grantha must
mean a written or bound book. In ancient times barks
and leaves of particular trees were used as writing materials for want of paper. The Bhúrja-pattra and palm leaves
were especially preferred. And even to this day Bhúrja-
pattra and palm leaves are used for writing purposes. In
Egypt this practice was also prevalent; and the very word
paper is derived from 'papyrus' which means the bark of
a reed.

The Srauta-Sútras of A'svaláyana and the Prátisákhyas
of the different Vedas contain numerous statements which
cannot be explained without admitting a knowledge of
letters on the part of the authors of those ancient works.
Admitting that there is no allusion in the Vaidik
hymns to writing, reading, paper, pen or anything else
connected with writing this can never be a conclusive
proof of the ignorance of the art of writing in ancient
India. How were the gigantic works of ancient times
divided into chapters and sections without any help of
writing? How without a knowledge of numerals were
the cattle marked on their ears in order to identify them?

[*] Manu, ch. 77.

Pāṇini has a *sûtra* (vi. 3, 115) in which he says that
the owners of cattle were at his time in the habit of
marking their beasts on the ears, with signs of a svastika
or magic figure of prosperity, a ladle, a pearl, &c.,
and also eight and five, which certainly point to a
knowledge of written letters or numerals at that period.
Similarly the use of *lopa*, to express elision,* as opposed to the visibility of a letter points to language
as existing in a written and not exclusively spoken form.
It is impossible that an author could speak of a thing
visible, literally or metaphorically, unless it were referable
to his sense of sight. A letter which has undergone the
effect of *lopa*, must, therefore, previously to its *lopa*, have
been a visible or written letter to him. Every one must
now understand that Pāṇini was as proficient in writing
as the cowherds of his time. It will not also be rash to
hold that the Vedas were preserved in writing at or before
Pāṇini's time. And it could be easily shown that Pāṇini
must have seen written Vaidik texts.† Now, it is obvious
that the ancient Hindūs must have been acquainted with
the art of writing. No question can be raised against the
fact that the Hindūs were acquainted with the art of
writing before the time of Alexander ; and the expressions
likhita and *likhāpita*‡ occur in the inscriptions of Piyadasi,
which are, no doubt, of the third century B. C. However,
we shall not exceed a reasonable limit by assigning the
13th century B. C. to the origin of writing in India.

* Pāṇini, i. 1, 60 : वर्तलोपे लोपः ।

† Pāṇini, vi. 1, 76 : हलन्त्यम् उपदेशे ।

‡ Manu, viii. 168.

What was the alphabet that Pánini and his predecessors used, is a question that can hardly be answered positively since there are not sufficient data to decide it. But it was by no means the Bactrian. The Bactrian is avowedly not full. Its vowels are few and at the same time not perfect, and even its consonants are deficient. In such a case the Bactrian could have been, by no means, originally adopted and used for a language most noted for its long and short vowels. To suppose that when a nation had once caught the idea of alphabetic writing, they would afterwards fail to devise a sufficient number of letters to meet their requirements, is quite absurd. It is also said that they must have got their alphabet from the Dravidians who were autochthonous in India ; and from no other source. But there is nothing to prove that these aborigines had a written literature at the time when the Aryans intruded on them and settled here. But even now has a single Dravidian book been discovered, which may be considered to be of a pre-Vaidik era. The Dravidians were by no means a literary race, their ancient history is quite a blank ; and the little that we know of them is from the writings of the Indo-Aryans themselves. That when the Dravidians themselves had no alphabet of their own, the Indo-Aryans borrowed one from them, is so illogical that it scarcely calls for farther notion. It is supposed by some that the Aryans did not originate an alphabet either before they migrated to India or after they settled here ; but they must have borrowed elsewhere. According to them the writing of the Indo-Aryans is of Semitic

origin.* Assuming that they came to India before they
had devised a system of alphabetic writing, it will not
be paradoxical to hazard an opinion (more especially
when they are said to have left their primitive home
in a far more advanced social state than their predecessors who had long before separated from them, and
gone forth in other directions,) that such a highly intellectual race as the Indo-Aryans would originate it in their
adopted country, without borrowing it from their neigh-
bours.

* Dunloy, Indian &c. Essh and Graber's Encyclopedia, 1846) p. 216 ;
Weber's Indische Skizzen (1858). p. 127 f ; and Burnell's biturouts of
South Indian Palæography, p. 9 ff.

APPENDIX.

The PURUSHA-SUKTA, or the 90th Hymn of the 10th Book of the Rig-veda Sanhitá.

1. Purusha has a thousand heads, a thousand eyes, a thousand feet. On every side enveloping the earth, he overpassed (it) by a space of ten fingers. 2. Purusha himself is this whole (universe), whatever has been and whatever shall be. He is also the lord of immortality, since (or, when) by food he expands. 3. Such is his greatness, and Purusha is superior to this. All existences are a quarter of him; and three-fourths of him are that which is immortal in the sky. 4. With three quarters Purusha mounted upwards. A quarter of him was again produced here. He was then diffused everywhere over things which eat and things which do not eat. 5. From him was born Virāj, and from Virāj, Purusha. When born, he extended beyond the earth, both behind and before. 6. When the gods performed a sacrifice with Purusha as the oblation, the spring was its butter, the summer its fuel, and the autumn its (accompanying) offering. 7. This victim, Purusha, born in the beginning, they immolated on the

sacrificial grass. With him the gods, the Sádhyas, and the rishis sacrificed. 8. From that universal sacrifice were provided curds and butter. It formed those aerial (creatures) and animals both wild and tame. 9. From that universal sacrifice sprang the rich-, sáman-, and chhandas-, verses: from it sprang the rajes. 10. From it sprang horses, and all animals with two rows of teeth; kine sprang from it; from it goats and sheep. 11. When (the gods) divided Purusha, into how many parts did they cut him up? what was his mouth? what arms (had he)? what (two objects) are said (to have been) his thighs and feet? 12. The Brahman was his mouth; the Rájanya was made his arms; the being (called) the Vaisya, he was his thighs; the Súdra sprang from his feet. 13. The moon sprang from his soul (manas), the sun from his eye, Indra and Agni from his mouth, and Váyu from his breath. 14. From his navel arose the air, from his head the sky, from his feet the earth, from his ear the (four) quarters: in this manner (the gods) formed the worlds. 15. When the gods, performing sacrifice, bound Purusha as a victim, there were seven sticks (stuck up) for it (around the fire), and thrice seven pieces of fuel were made. 16. With sacrifice the gods performed the sacrifice. These were the earliest rites. These great powers have sought the sky, where are the former Sádhyas, gods.

JOHN MUIR.

www.ingramcontent.com/pod-product-compliance
Lightning Source LLC
Chambersburg PA
CBHW020537270326
41927CB00006B/622